SCRIPT
tease

DEDICATION

For Eleanor

SCRIPT
tease

Today's Hottest Screenwriters Bare All

DYLAN CALLAGHAN

Avon, Massachusetts

Published by
Adams Media, a division of F+W Media, Inc.
57 Littlefield Street, Avon, MA 02322. U.S.A.
www.adamsmedia.com

ISBN 10: 1-4405-4077-2
ISBN 13: 978-1-4405-4077-6
eISBN 10: 1-4405-4176-0
eISBN 13: 978-1-4405-4176-6

Printed in the United States of America.

10 9 8 7 6 5 4 3 2 1

Library of Congress Cataloging-in-Publication Data
Callaghan, Dylan.
  Script tease / Dylan Callaghan.
    p. cm.
  "The interviews included within this book were originally published
by the Writers Guild of America, West, on its website, *www.wga.org.*"
  ISBN 978-1-4405-4077-6 (pbk.) – ISBN 1-4405-4077-2 (pbk.) –
ISBN 978-1-4405-4176-6 (ebook) – ISBN 1-4405-4176-0 (ebook)
  1. Motion picture authorship. 2. Screen writers–Interviews. I. Title.
  PN1996.C295 2012
  809.2'3–dc23
                        2012026392

The interviews included within this book were originally published
by the Writers Guild of America, West, on its website, *www.wga.org*.

Many of the designations used by manufacturers and sellers to
distinguish their product are claimed as trademarks. Where those
designations appear in this book and Adams Media was aware of a
trademark claim, the designations have been printed with initial capital
letters.

This book is available at quantity discounts for bulk purchases.
For information, please call 1-800-289-0963.

CONTENTS

INTRODUCTION

"No man but a blockhead ever wrote except for money."
—SAMUEL JOHNSON

The reason most screenwriters fail is something Elmore Leonard touches on in this book when he cites the above Samuel Johnson quote: wanting to get paid and paid well for one's writing is absolutely righteous and correct. But you have to also understand that money does not and cannot matter if you want to write a good movie script.

That is a central lesson articulated repeatedly in this compendium of candid interviews with over two dozen of the best screenwriters on the planet.

It's good to take a class, great to attend a writer's workshop, and, of course, fantastic to buy a really great book on the subject (there are only a few!). But none of these activities matter if you don't roll up the old shirtsleeves and get dirty—bang out pages, write scripts, and learn what the form does in your own unique hands.

These interviews brim with powerful and rare insights from today's smartest scripters, but they won't help you if you aren't willing to open yourself up to the joy and brutality of the process itself. Do the work and do it on stories that you're truly invested in or, simply put, you can be almost certain you won't succeed.

Take screenwriter Allan Loeb. In these pages he tells the raw truth about how he toiled for twelve years trying to write scripts he thought would sell rather than ones he was passionate about. He wound up penniless, dropped by his agent, and plagued by a nasty gambling addiction.

The very same day he got dumped by his agent, he followed the corniest advice in the writing business: He wrote what was in his heart. He had wanted to write the resulting script, *The Only Living Boy in New York*, for years, but he feared it wasn't commercial.

Overnight *Living Boy*, whose title comes from a Simon and Garfunkel tune, got him inked to Creative Artists Agency. It sold in a month and landed him on an insiders' list of hot screenwriters that circulates among Hollywood powerbrokers.

Not everybody is Allan Loeb, and that fact brings up another prevailing lesson here: each successful scripter's path is his or her own. Whether it's Oscar winner Eric Roth, who can spend months working and reworking his first twenty or so pages before he knows where he's going, or the Italian Stallion, Sly Stallone, who literally painted his apartment windows black to write *Rocky*, these interviews are the Comstock Lode of wisdom from the screenwriting trenches.

As varied as the subjects here are, as different as their styles and approaches, they're unified by both the idea that real work inside the screenwriting craft is mandatory for success and that theory and formula author nothing.

Oscar-nominated screenwriter Steve Kloves (*Wonder Boys*), who penned all but one of the *Harry Potter* films—the most successful film franchise in history—says that even from script to script in a single franchise, there's no formula. Every story has its own singular set of keys.

All the screenwriters included here are like eyewitnesses to the same spectacular event. They each observed different illuminating details, but the basic truth of what they all saw proves remarkably consistent.

Finally, it should be noted that all these storytellers are themselves great stories. They are from disparate corners, from rich parents and poor, with PhDs and narrowly earned high school diplomas. But they've all gotten dirty, written and rewritten many pages, and trudged through the darkness of the creative process to find the light.

DARREN ARONOFSKY

CAREER HIGHLIGHTS:
Black Swan; The Wrestler; Pi; Requiem for a Dream

"I'm kind of a nomadic writer. I like to write in a certain place for a week or two and then I've gotta move somewhere else . . . My sacred sanctuary is always changing."

—DARREN ARONOFSKY

Ever since he rocketed out of the blue into the stratosphere of indie film with 1998's *Pi*, Darren Aronofsky has been, among other things, an exemplar of the idea that creative success comes through never repeating yourself. During a discussion about his beautifully fabulistic foray into the world of sci-fi love stories, *The Fountain*, the Harvard-educated Brooklynite talks about everything from his writing process to his love for the *Matrix* films.

He says that despite being such a visually inclined director, when he is writing, the visual stuff rarely comes into play. And though he loves playing with narrative and genre boundaries, he believes ardently that, no matter how fascinating experimentation is, every successful screenplay's journey begins with a great story.

You've said that it's very difficult to know exactly where ideas start. What is your first clear recollection of the idea for _The Fountain_ emerging?

I think it was after seeing _The Matrix_ about two weeks before we started shooting _Requiem for a Dream._ I saw it and I realized that it was time to do something completely different and new in sci-fi. That was the challenge I set in front of myself.

At the same time, a roommate of mine from college, Ari Handel, had just gotten his PhD in neuroscience and was done with academia. He was interested in writing so I asked him to think about doing something completely new with sci-fi. The two of us started walking around Manhattan thinking and talking and one of the first concepts was [using] the fountain of youth as a starting point. We felt a search for immortality would allow us to do something that spanned time in a different way than a traditional time-travel movie.

But _The Matrix_ kind of got the ball rolling?

Yeah, I think so. I was a fan of sci-fi and felt that the Wachowski brothers had taken most of the great sci-fi ideas of the twentieth century and added a bunch of new ones as well, [and] that it was time to do something very different. That gave us the idea to move away from films about outer space and start doing films about inner space.

And would you say that the focus on inner space is what defines this movie?

> Yeah. I think sci-fi in movies has really been hijacked by laser guns, gadgetry, and gimmicks like that. We decided to move away from that. For instance our space bubble is a spaceship that's not at all connected to spaceships from other films. We wanted to get away from jet propulsion and, you know, basically trucks in space.

You've called this film a puzzle and it does span 1,000 years and three different time periods—without being reductive, can you tell me what, in the simplest sense, this story is about?

> At the core it's a love story between Hugh Jackman and Rachel Weisz. Rachel's character has terminal brain cancer and is facing an untimely death. Hugh Jackman's character is a research scientist doing work with cancer. He has a possibility of saving her and refuses to accept what's happening to [her].

And in that sense refuses to accept mortality?

> Exactly.

INTERVIEWER

As a writer-director you're a visual artist—you have certain key techniques you use in your films: your treatment of sound, montage, etc. When you write are you perpetually visualizing the filmic expression of the words?

DARREN ARONOFSKY

Not always. I think there are certain things that come to me with cool visuals attached, but most of the time when you're a writer, you're a writer, and you're just trying to figure out how the scenes work. Then at a certain point you have to take off your writer's cap and put on your director's cap and figure out how you visually execute what you've created on the page. When you're writing, the essential focus is not the visual aspect but just the best way to do a scene.

Do you have any quirky rituals for the actual writing process?

> I'm kind of a nomadic writer. I like to write in a certain place for a week or two and then I've gotta move somewhere else.

So you don't have a sacred sanctuary?

> No, my sacred sanctuary is always changing.

As a kind of new-wave storyteller who defies convention, how do you navigate the perilous chasm between reinvention and the basic engines of good storytelling?

> There's a constant pull between trying to do something new and trying to keep it understandable for audiences. You don't want to go too far out there where audiences don't get what's going on, but you want to keep things fresh. There's always going to be people who don't want to see something so new, but I think there're always more people who want to have their minds blown.

How do you know when you've gone too far?

> Your first responsibility is to get the story across; if you're not getting a story across then you're doing a disservice to the audience. The bottom line is that a good story must be there, but if the audience is on the ride, then why not push it a little further?

SHANE BLACK

CAREER HIGHLIGHTS:

Kiss, Kiss, Bang, Bang; Lethal Weapon; The Long Kiss Goodnight; Last Action Hero

---

"People have asked, aren't you afraid? I've said, 'Fuck it, no!' [*laughs*] I have nothing to lose. How could it get worse? No one knew my name anymore, who the fuck I was or that I was even still alive . . . So I just jumped in."

—SHANE BLACK

When scripting vet Shane Black talks about screenwriting, it's existential, brutal, and you can bet, pretty much bang on. He set the bar for a new era of mega screenwriting paydays when, in 1996, he was paid a jaw-slacking $4 million for *The Long Kiss Goodnight*, which ultimately didn't perform at the box office. He suffered a backlash that sent him into the wilderness.

Here he talks Raymond Chandler, badly written blockbusters, and coming back from Hollywood's Siberia. When you are working, he says, make "every day the same" and your writing will build momentum. Also, be sure to keep a shoebox where you put every idea you ever have.

What do you feel *Kiss, Kiss, Bang, Bang* represents in relation to your earlier screenwriting credits?

I think *Kiss, Kiss, Bang, Bang* is sort of the bastard child of James L. Brooks and Joel Silver, both of whom were very influential in getting me to write this thing. I took lessons from both of them as I wrote it. It's half romantic comedy tempered with murder mystery that's edgy and, at points, I think, even disturbing.

It's also a departure from doing mythic, iconic characters like Mel Gibson's gunslinger in *Lethal Weapon* and Geena Davis's female avenger in *The Long Kiss Goodnight*—characters writ large, as they say. In this one the mythic figure is sensed but never seen in the Johnny Gossamer character that sort of floats through the movie as an ideal to be attained. But the people trying to fill his shoes are these schmucks who can't. It's one of the first movies I've done where the people are just people.

The [Robert] Downey character may be a hero with pimples, so to speak, but he still winds up hanging from a corpse's arm over an L.A. freeway shooting bad guys with his free hand.

That's the idea of the movie, that there are no mythical characters until the very end when he actually changes reality. In order to save this girl and rekindle that childhood love he has.

That "magic" [Downey's character is seen as a child magician in flashback] . . .

> Yeah, it's actual magic. He becomes Johnny Gossamer. That's the idea. That's why he's able to hang onto a woman's arm and kill eight people.

The film pays obvious homage to classic detective noir, even using Raymond Chandler titles for act breaks. About his own screenwriting, Chandler said, "If my books had been any worse I should not have been invited to Hollywood and if they had been any better I should not have come." What are your thoughts about that?

> I find the idea of writing a novel as daunting as anyone. I think there's a specific format in screenwriting that you can take in so many directions. You only have 120 pages to deal with, so every word is precious.
>
> In a 1,000-page Tom Wolfe novel, it may be great, but it's a fucking thousand pages! If I talk for five hours without stopping, I'm probably going to say something interesting. But if you only have a certain space, it's like a Tetris game. You've got to get as many thoughts and ideas, character bits, jokes, drama—you've gotta stuff it in there and leave no spaces. So I kept arranging and rearranging the elements in this script until I had stuffed as much story into as little space as I could. That's what I think is the unique challenge of screenplays.

What is your process when penning a script? Are you a ritualistic, obsessive-compulsive type or . . . ?

I'm an obsessive compulsive, but that doesn't translate to any consistency in terms of applying myself. I actually took an idea from a very good writer, Pen Densham (*Moll Flanders*, *Robin Hood: Prince of Thieves*). What Pen does and what I started to do is that every time I have a scrap of dialogue or an idea or a theme, I throw it in a shoebox. After a period of six or eight months I dump out the shoebox and start sifting through. Sometimes you don't even remember stuff you've written, but what you're looking for is the thread that emerges. Hopefully you'll get a loose idea.

And when you actually start honing that loose idea, what's your routine?

It's miserable. I try to make every day the same. I'll try to get myself five days in a row of uninterrupted time where I don't have friends coming over, I don't have people with problems calling me. And then I just get up, have breakfast, look at notes, go for a long walk, come back, maybe type a scene for three hours, take a break, have some lunch, take another walk, and come back and hone and revise the scene, maybe make some notes for the next day . . . but you have it all mapped out. You just do it the same way every day. What happens is, you gain a momentum. You're alone, but you're engrossed.

What appeals to you about quick, cynical humor and the buddy-movie archetype?

I think that that kind of pithy throwaway stuff is the kind of humor I've always enjoyed, but beyond that, [as far as] friendships and partners, I've always liked these sort of movies where people come together for a time and then at the end they part or whatever. But you feel like you've been on a journey with them. That's the feeling that I've always loved and tried to get at with these movies. The ride is better with two people than with just one, or it has always seemed so to me. Friendships are really all there is.

INTERVIEWER

If *Lethal Weapon* was a defining hit of the late eighties, what do you think stylistically makes a winning script today?

SHANE BLACK

I don't see many winning screenplays these days, unless you go to the indie world. To me, character-driven screenplays make you turn the page because you're desperately invested in what happens to the characters. I don't see them much anymore. The blockbusters tend to be poorly written. I do like the *X-Men* movies, by the way.

But in general, when I go to see a big action movie nowadays, I don't like it . . . The Charlie Kaufmans and the *21 Grams*–type movies, those are the movies that are interesting. The scripts that are getting all the acclaim are by the eclectic writers who take an odd tactic, who take a sort of oblique approach. The ones that try to be accessible and blockbustery tend not to work.

IAN BRENNAN AND BRAD FALCHUK

CAREER HIGHLIGHTS:
Glee; Nip/Tuck

"As long as we focus on the writing and these characters, the music will keep selling. But the second it becomes a music video, then it doesn't have any meaning to it."

—BRAD FALCHUK

Ian Brennan literally used *Screenwriting for Dummies* to write his first-ever feature script. It was called *Glee* and, even though it became a TV show instead of a movie, it's fair to say it worked.

With the help of writer-producers Ryan Murphy and Brad Falchuk, Brennan turned his originally darker feature script—based partially on his experience in show choir at Prospect High School in Illinois—into one of the biggest TV series of the new millennium.

Brennan and Falchuk say that they spend the bulk of their writing time pitching plot beats back and forth (often in the luxury of Hollywood's posh Chateau Marmont), rather than rewriting. That makes for the strongest scripts, they say. And, as massively gargantuan as the show has become through the use of popular music, both writers insist story must come first, never the other way around.

How did this all coalesce and you guys all come together with Ryan Murphy?

Ian Brennan: I had an idea for a movie and it ended up with Ryan and Brad, and they said it might make a good TV show. So I went in and met them and we clicked right away. We went right into making a pilot, and here it is, probably twenty months later.

So this has been whirlwind for you in particular?

Ian Brennan: Crazy. It feels like I'm living someone else's life. Wonderful.

Tell me how the writing on this show works for you two on a daily basis. What's the rough recipe for breaking and turning around episodes?

The process is basically that Ian, Ryan, and I come up with a basic theme or premise for an episode, and we'll start pitching ideas and breaking story from that point. There's a lot of pitching and back and forth that goes on between the three of us.

Ryan has a very quick ability to take a lot of information and hone it down to simple beats for a story. So we may have pitched out twelve beats and he'll be able to say, "Hold on," and write down a nine- or ten-beat story.

The process tends to go pretty quickly. We meet up Sunday nights—we go to the Chateau Marmont for dinner and talk about what the next episode is going to be. We start gathering our beats and then break those out into acts, and then we start writing scenes. Then we put them all together, and there's very little rewriting that goes on once you get to that point. There's cutting and a joke pass to punch it up a little bit, but that's usually about it.

With this show do you always have the beats of the plot and fit the songs to it or does it ever work the other way around?

By and large the music always comes out of the writing. We'll know the story and the scenes first. And normally we just know, "Oh, the song that needs to go here is *blank*," you know? We've been incredibly lucky getting the music we want. It's been shocking. I think we have a success rate of about 95 percent. And we're now in a position where artists are kind of courting us.

Aren't you guys being deluged?

Brad Falchuk: A little bit but it's a high-class problem to have. We know that . . . we start with the concept and the story, and it all comes out of the story. [In a way] we don't have to worry about being, I don't know, corrupted by some artist's insistent manager.

INTERVIEWER
With the music industry being more
ravenous for exposure than ever,
do you feel as if there's any danger
down the line of the show's writing
and narrative soul being affected by
the music?

BRAD FALCHUK
That's our job, to keep the integrity
of the show pure. We're fortunate
that our corporate partners are so
supportive they would never dare
do that. They understand how the
show works. The songs that sell the
best are the songs that are involved
in the strongest story lines and writing. So the idea of coming the other
way around and saying, "Let's find
an emotional way to use this song,"
would not work.

I think they realize that and we realize that. As long as we focus on the
writing and these characters, the
music will keep selling. But the second it becomes a music video, then it
doesn't have any meaning to it.

The writing is definitely the ball you want to keep your eyes on here?

Brad Falchuk: Absolutely. What happens with the best film and TV music is that you watch a scene and hear a song, and you can no longer hear that song without thinking of that scene and those characters.

Ian, I'm curious, from your original conception of this as a film, what has most surprised you about how this idea, this story, has worked as a produced piece?

Ian Brennan: I think what has surprised me about the show throughout—from the writing of the pilot to now—is its capacity for heart, which sounds weird. I think of the three of us, I have the most cynical mind about the subject matter. I was in show choir, and I have a more biting sense of it all. I'm amazed every time we come up with a script how much heart is in it without it ever seeming sappy.

To what extent do you guys think that in these sober times of economic strife and war there is more of an appetite for the kind of heart, sweetness, and positivity you see in this show and other new shows like *Modern Family*, whereas darkness and edge was the zeitgeist a couple years ago?

Brad Falchuk: I think our attitude was to give the show snark and edge without any cynicism. We beat people up pretty good, and our characters get beat up pretty good. They're tortured the way high school kids are, but there's never any hopelessness or cynicism in it.

I don't know if that's a sign of the times. It feels to me like a more mature kind of comedy in a way. It's not laughing at people, it's laughing with them and saying, "That was me too. I felt that way and I get it." Much more of the John Hughes and Judd Apatow kind of humor.

Where do you guys see this show going?

Brad Falchuk: We've aired thirteen episodes, and we're just about to start shooting our sixteenth. You think about TV shows and when they find their stride, this show is still cold, you know? We're just starting to figure this out. I'm really excited to find out what happens with these characters in a third season.

Ian Brennan: I don't know. This is such a dream. It's the kind of dream you don't dare voice, it's been that amazing. I don't care what happens, I just want it to go on forever.

DIABLO CODY

CAREER HIGHLIGHTS:

Juno; *Young Adult*; *United States of Tara*

"I'm not really qualified to give any advice at all, but when I meet people and they absolutely demand some random pearl of wisdom, I always tell them to be comfortable in their own skin and to just fucking unclench. I'm sorry, there's never been a great writer that wasn't fucked up. Writers are fucked-up drunks; that's just the way it goes. Embrace it."

—DIABLO CODY

For Diablo Cody, chaos is the mother of invention. The erstwhile stripper and blogger turned Oscar-winning screenwriter likes to ride her creative mojo where it goes.

During an expansive chat about *United States of Tara*, she talks *Juno*, rebuts the haters, and says not outlining, not planning, and not deciding where a story goes is the best way to write a good one.

"I'm not an architect of surprises," she explains. Her characters are ultimately in charge. She's just as surprised about where they wind up as you.

Is it fortunate happenstance that you're following up an Oscar-winning feature script debut with a TV project or is it a good way to juke the whole expectations thing?

Yeah, I have said that. It's a nice buffer. I wasn't sure what would be out first, *Jennifer's Body,* which is shockingly different than *Juno* . . .

That's your next feature, a horror film, right?

Yeah, or this show. I was pleased that it was this show in terms of timing and expectations. I don't like to buy into the whole "sophomore jinx" thing. They ask me if I feel any pressure and I don't know what they're talking about. I already have an Oscar. I'm just gonna coast from here on out.

If I didn't have an Oscar, then I would feel that intense, gnawing pressure, but I don't.

No one can touch you now?

No, I don't think that's true. There are a lot of people that can touch me. But I just think backwards. Now that I achieved something that a lot of people reach for, I can do things that are interesting to me.

You can relax a little bit.

I can relax a little bit. I feel very fortunate.

You have obviously met with amazing success, but with that success has come a fair amount of snarkage, as you call it. A recurring snark has been that either your dialogue is not realistic for a teenage girl . . .

> Yeah, that's why I won an Oscar—because my dialogue is bad.

Look, I'm not saying this, it's just something you read. They also say that your characters tend to sound the same. Is that total bullshit?

> Actually, I have never heard the criticism that my characters sound the same. Have not heard that one. That is new.

Oh, shit.

> It's fine. It's obviously not true. If you just compare *Juno* and *United States of Tara* . . . yeah, I really see the similarity there.

That's true. This show could not be a more pointed demonstration of different voices for different characters.

> I like writing stylized dialogue. I have had a really unique career trajectory because I'm willing to have a signature style, you know what I mean? Everybody always says, "Writers don't get to go on talk shows." That's because a lot of writers are hired guns who are just doing what people want them to do. I'm willing to offend some people's sensibilities to get noticed.

INTERVIEWER
Is your unique voice something that
just happened or did you cultivate it?

DIABLO CODY
I don't know. I'm the same person
I've always been. Honestly, I don't
understand it. If you go on the Internet there are thousands of unknown
bloggers who are funnier than me,
more outspoken or better writers
than me. I don't know why I was
chosen. I don't. I don't really think I
have that distinct a persona. Snark
is universal.

I just think I've been really lucky,
I have good timing and I'm good at
exploiting situations.

But you are funny. It's maybe overlooked a bit. What have been some crucial influences on your sense of humor?

I know this might seem like an unlikely influence, but I like Woody Allen.

No, that doesn't seem that weird.

And, I'm sorry, but every day I find ten people to laugh at, just in public. People are hilarious. Things people say to each other unironically are hilarious. The world is full of material.

That's what's strange to me. I think actual human beings have more interesting conversations than some of the ones I typically hear on television. I don't understand why writing would be more boring than life. It should be the other way around.

How much is your style based on just being a keen observer?

A lot of it. All I do is sit and watch people. All I do is sort of rip off the human condition.

I guess I feel like writers kind of forget about the connective tissue. I want to make every line count—every one, even if it's just exposition. I think that's what lends the hyper-real quality, the fact that when real people announce that they're going to the bathroom, they don't make it that interesting, whereas I like to.

So it's real-life observations on steroids?

Yeah, exactly. Real life on steroids is a good description.

Your dialogue, like your blog, has a tangential, free-form rhythm. How are you at structure?

Thing is, I don't outline. I just sit down and make up a story and then flesh it out into a script.

What guides you through a story if you don't outline? Is it character or a certain voice?

I like to pick a theme. I know that sounds stupid. It's not a super advanced technique. They pick a theme on *Laverne and Shirley.* I think about what the emotional core of the story is, what's something I can play on across multiple story lines, and then I go from there.

I like to come up with the theme and play with variations on it.

There is something you did incredibly well in *Juno* and *Tara* as well: You flip characters from their initial position. In *Juno*, for example, the initially unlikable, uptight, wanna-be mom Vanessa ends up true and heroic in a way, whereas the funny husband you like at first turns out to be a selfish, kinda pathetic turd.

How deliberately do you design your character arcs that way and why?

It's not premeditated, believe me! I wish I was like this master craftsman who could do those things on purpose. I'm no Shyamalan; I'm not an architect of surprises. In the case of Vanessa in *Juno*, I wound up liking her more and more as I wrote the script and my own sympathies shifted. I went on the same journey as the viewers. I definitely didn't start out thinking, "Vanessa is a stealth heroine." I initially thought she was really annoying, and I planned to roast her from beginning to end. I was on Team Mark all the way. But Vanessa won me over, and the plot began to shift in her favor. That's the cool part of writing, getting assimilated into the story.

So much has been made about the snappy, cynical tone of your writing, but there seems to be this kind of sweet candy center to your stories. Is that fair?

Yeah, definitely. I never realized that I could appeal to peoples' emotions until *Juno* came out and I saw people crying in the theater. I thought, "Oh my God, I had no idea you could tweak people that easily." I quickly realized that sentimentality is a good thing to have in your arsenal. People love sweet shit, they just do. They eat that shit up. They want to hear life-affirming stories.

Do you eat that stuff up?

> Not necessarily. It often surprises me that I wrote a so-called emotional movie, although I usually blame Jason Reitman for that. I'm actually pretty cynical. I relate more to people who hate my writing than to people who love it, if that makes any sense.

You relate to the people who hate your writing more?

> Yeah, because the people who hate my writing are usually kind of mean spirited. I don't know how to put this; I'm not a mean-spirited person, but I am a little more cynical than you might think based on my writing.

You seem cynical, but what about the idea that every cynic is a true sentimentalist or idealist inside?

> Is that true? I've never heard that before, that a cynic is a true idealist?

In the sense that cynicism is a kind of protection?

> That's probably true. Every cynic is probably an adorable porcupine shielding itself, you know what I mean?

Yeah, I know what you mean—adorable porcupine.

I'm just shooting spines everywhere. No, but I do have
sincere affection for Tara and her family. I didn't want to
see bad things happen to them, and I didn't want to see
bad things happen to Juno. I do care about my characters. But I'm often surprised by how mushy things can
get in the third act.

**As cynical as you are, you're also comfortable with your
own "treacliness," right? If the third act gets mushy,
you're cool with it, right?**

Sure. I mean, I've seen *Waiting to Exhale* like twenty-
five times. Besides, even cool people like Wes Anderson
write mushy stuff from time to time. *The Royal Tenen-
baums* is like *One Life to Live* with tracksuits.

Give me an idea of how many hours you put in each week.

I work in bursts, so there are some that are zero and
some where I put in a normal workweek that an actual
human being would work.

And the rest of the time you walk around being cynical?

Yeah, you can tell that is such complete bullshit. I call
myself a cynic, but I'm such a liar . . . But honestly, my
working patterns are very erratic, and I hope they stay

that way. The day that I actually become consistent, I'll know my heart's dead.

So, in a way, do you feel like if you become consistent and you lose the chaos, your writing will die?

Absolutely. My writing is the writing of a person who cannot organize their thoughts. The day that I become a hyper-functional human being is the day that I won't write anymore.

That's great. You're going to help a lot of people with that advice.

I'm not really qualified to give any advice at all, but when I meet people and they absolutely demand some random pearl of wisdom, I always tell them to be comfortable in their own skin and to just fucking unclench. I'm sorry, there's never been a great writer that wasn't fucked up. Writers are fucked-up drunks, that's just the way it goes. Embrace it.

You know, people are like, "Oh, I want to be creative and I also want to be a good person." And I'm like, "Uh, uh, not gonna work."

So are you not a good person, Diablo?

I'm a wonderful person morally, but in terms of . . . I
don't think you understand what I'm getting at. Like, I
don't pick up my clothes, this is what I'm trying to say.
My clothes are on the floor and have been for months . . .

I get it—you live in chaos.

I live in chaos. I'm a type-B individual, I cannot tell
you where any of my scripts are. In fact I don't own a
printer. I just kind of live in squalor and that's not necessarily a bad thing.

JOEL AND ETHAN COEN

CAREER HIGHLIGHTS:

No Country for Old Men; Fargo; The Big Lebowski; Blood Simple

---

Joel Coen: [Early on in writing *O Brother, Where Art Thou?*] we didn't know we were adapting *The Odyssey*.

Ethan Coen: That's an interesting screenwriting phenomenon; when you're doing an adaptation but aren't aware of it.

Joel Coen: For Christ's sake, it's *The Odyssey*!

Ethan Coen: Yeah, at some point we looked at each other and said . . .

Joel Coen: "Call someone and find out if the rights are available!"

Filmmaking brothers Ethan and Joel Coen have, somewhat quietly, created one of the richest bodies of film in history. They are as literate as they are laconic, as funny and unassuming as they are cranky. But get them going on screenwriting and the brainy writing geeks emerge. In a wide-ranging sit-down for *True Grit,* they start out a tad cranky, but wind up geeking out, dishing good knowledge about everything from *Miller's Crossing* and *Fargo* to *No Country for Old Men.*

Like the fact that all through their careers, they have never out-lined. They just try to know what the next step is, and it works out. It's why, for example, they are massive fans of Dashiell Hammett's novels, but feel his overly complex plots don't work for screenplays.

Perhaps most important, the Coen brothers say, if you get stuck on a script, just walk away.

How long were you writing *True Grit*?

> *Ethan Coen*: Not terribly long. As you know, or might know, it's a fairly faithful adaptation.

How much of the dialogue is directly from [Charles] Portis's novel?

> *Ethan Coen*: At least three quarters or more. I don't know, most.

They are, in many ways, totally disparate stories, but to what extent do *No Country* and *True Grit* feel like they're in a similar ether?

> *Joel Coen*: Not at all.

On the face of it, they are not so similar, but I was just curious if creatively they came from a similar place at all.

> *Ethan Coen*: No, really. It's funny, I kind of want to say yes, but not as a writing thing. They're both kind of exterior movies and weather movies.

So visually?

> *Ethan Coen*: Yeah, more of a production thing.

> *Joel Coen*: What links them in our, or in *my* mind anyway, like you were saying before, they're both adapta-

tions of books that don't need a lot of embellishment or decoration from the book [to script]. They're both [cases where] we felt there's nothing wrong with the book. The idea is to do the book, not to do something else.

To not screw up the book?

Joel Coen: To not screw up the book, right.

Are there any quick pros and cons of the adaptation process for you guys?

Joel Coen: The pros are the obvious one; that you have this guide. If it's a novel like *True Grit* or Cormac's [McCarthy] novel [*No Country for Old Men*] or *To the White Sea*, which is an adaptation we did of a James Dickey novel, the exercise is to, as you said, not screw up the novel, to do the novel. You have something that is the essential guide to the whole thing, which you don't have with other scripts.

I guess the main con is the obvious one too; that there are things that can be achieved in a literary format that aren't necessarily achievable [in film]. It isn't a one-to-one correspondence between a novel and what you might do in a movie, or it may even be antithetical to what you can do in a movie and you have to find a solution for that.

Then there's the editing aspect; you can't put everything in.

Any great sacrifices you had to make?

Ethan Coen: Kind of, and actually, [and] here's a point of similarity with [*No Country for Old Men*]. Cormac's book is told in first person—well, actually it kind of checkerboards the first-person monologues of the sheriff with third-person omniscient. [But] we knew, sadly, that we'd lose some of the humor and digressiveness of those first-person monologues because you just can't carry on to that degree in a movie with voiceover.

Similarly [with *True Grit*], part of the power of the story and character is derived from the digressive and often very funny things [Mattie Ross, the film's young female protagonist] says in her first-person narration. You're aware in both cases that you're losing a lot and you're just trying to put those points across, to the extent that you can, in dramatic scenes as opposed to interior monologues.

Joel Coen: And you're trying to get the flavor of it, because the flavor of the novel is so much her voice.

Ethan Coen: That really is a strong a similarity between the two processes, in terms of writing, that is peculiar to these two novels because they are so interesting as first-person narration.

You guys generally don't outline, right?

Ethan Coen: Yeah.

INTERVIEWER
So with an adaptation, do you go
through and pick your plot points
and decide what scenes you're gonna
do or do you just plow through?

JOEL COEN
It's much more the case that there's
a discussion about what comes next
extending a certain way into the
script that often gets batted about
verbally and then just gets written
as opposed to writing it all down
with one subset of A, B, C, D, and E,
you know? It's like, "Okay, this will
happen and it will lead to this, and
then we don't know what."

ETHAN COEN
That's true. It's kinda mushy. We
don't do an outline in terms of mapping out the whole thing but then,
on the other hand, we don't exactly
write scene A and then stop and say,
"Okay, what's scene B?"

JOEL COEN
Yeah, it might be, "Okay, this will happen and lead to this and this and then
we get here and we'll figure it out."

It's kind of a floating outline?

> *Ethan Coen*: Yes, a floating outline. If we're writing
> scene B we have some clear idea of what scene C might
> be and a slightly fuzzier idea of what D might be and a
> vague idea of what the ramifications of that might be—
> or maybe not. It just kind of falls off into darkness.

**Don't you ever walk into the woods that way and find
yourself lost?**

> *Joel Coen*: Well, yeah, that's the classic thing. We joke
> about this all the time. When we were writing *Fargo*,
> we wrote the script to the point where it literally said
> "FADE IN: SHEP'S APARTMENT—Carl is humping
> the escort."
>
> It stayed that way for like four months. We would occa-
> sionally look at the last thing we wrote and that's what it
> said and we didn't know where it went from there. And
> we went off and did something else and eventually we
> somehow managed to write beyond that.
>
> *Ethan Coen*: On *O Brother, Where Art Thou?* we wrote
> through to, well, not very far. It begins with three
> escaped guys chained together and we wrote through
> what became George Clooney's monologue on the train
> to the hobos, and then we put it aside for three or four
> years and did a couple movies and came back to it.

SOFIA
COPPOLA

CAREER HIGHLIGHTS:

Lost in Translation; *Marie Antoinette*; *The Virgin Suicides*; *Somewhere*

"A lot of times in movies, it's big dramatic things like being held hostage or war that make people change. I wanted to do something more like in life where something little that doesn't seem like a big deal can really bring you to look at yourself and change."

—SOFIA COPPOLA

Sofia Coppola doesn't write explosions. She prefers the subtle, nonetheless tectonic shifting of real life—even a real life that tends to be a good deal more posh than most.

During a chat about her film *Somewhere* from a suite in the Four Seasons Hotel in Beverly Hills, she espoused the advantages of writing with a specific actor in mind. Little things that bring change to characters are the keys she loves to use to turn a plot. And, even though her dad loves to work early in the morning, and now that she's a mother she can't really stay up late, her creative heart still belongs to the night.

Though *Somewhere* is about a male movie star, this seems almost autobiographical. What do you think about that?

I feel like it's a personal film and I put a lot of myself into it, but I wouldn't say autobiographical because my life and childhood were so different than this story. But it is personal and I've put a lot of things I've seen and been around and imagined in there.

What makes it personal for you?

The life is so different but I feel like it's a world that I'm familiar with and that I've been around. I was trying to write about what was on my mind. I'd just had a baby so I was thinking about how being a parent changes your perspective. I imagined how that would be for this kind of a guy. I try to put myself into the character's point of view even though my life isn't like theirs.

What aspect of your being a mom is infused in this piece?

I guess I was just thinking about how having a kid changes you. I was imagining this guy having a kid, and I know what it's like to have a kid, but I can't imagine what it's like living that kind of lifestyle and having a kid and how your priorities must change. I tried to put what was important and on my mind into this.

Also, becoming a parent you look at your childhood. I tried to put memories of significant moments in the movie. When I was writing the father-daughter stuff, I tried to put in those memories.

Is there any of your dad in [Stephen Dorff's character]?

Not in Johnny Marco, just in the fun, sweet side of the dad with the kid. Johnny Marco is based on a bunch of different actors and rock stars all put together, but not on my dad.

I also read that Stephen Dorff came to your mind as the lead while you were writing. At what stage?

At the beginning, when I thought of this character I thought of Stephen. I always find it helpful when I'm writing to picture an actor.

It gives you a tone?

Yeah, it just helps you picture it. It gives a face to what you're imagining and how they would approach it.

Why Stephen? Not that there's anything wrong with him.

I had known Stephen over the years. Knowing him in real life, I thought he had a real sweet side that could bring a lot of heart to a character that's pretty flawed and make you care about him.

So the sweetness could kind of carry through any unlikable qualities?

Yeah, with another actor . . . this character is already in danger of people wondering why they would care about this guy.

When and where do you write now?

I used to stay up late at night and write all night because there were no distractions, no phone. I have little kids, so I can't stay up anymore. With this I would just kind of write in the afternoons when my daughter would go off to the park. I have a little office at home.

I'm not a morning person. My dad gets up really early and writes and I just can't.

So you don't feel that fresh creative power in the morning that people talk about?

No. I understand why people do that, but I don't. I kinda like to get things out of the way and then do it.

INTERVIEWER
I know music is important to this
film and to you in general. How much
do you either listen to music while
writing or does music give you ideas
for later writing?

SOFIA COPPOLA
I think both. I listen to music when
I'm writing. A lot of times I listen to
music that fits the mood, and then
some of that music will end up in the
movie. I think it's a combination of
using music to just space out and listening to it when I'm writing.

In a lot of your films and particularly in this one, there's this enticing, beautiful portrait of a place—in this case L.A.—but then there's also this isolation, coldness, and loneliness. Is this an intentional theme you try to get at or does it just manifest itself in your films?

I think it just comes out. I don't sit down intending to do that. I like stories about when people change. I feel like a lot of times in movies, it's big dramatic things like being held hostage or war that make people change. I wanted to do something more like in life where something little that doesn't seem like a big deal can really bring you to look at yourself and change.

EMILIO ESTEVEZ

CAREER HIGHLIGHTS:

The Way; Bobby; That Was Then . . . This Is Now

"Writing is perhaps the most difficult and lonely of the three jobs [directing, acting, and writing] because, there you are, all alone, and you've gotta come up with something. I'll tell you that I don't really like writing but I also love writing."

—EMILIO ESTEVEZ

As an actor, Emilio Estevez has been at the epicenter of hugely profitable big studio movies. But as a writer-director, he's as much of an outsider artist as anyone (almost). Talking about his film *Bobby*, he says writers don't get the respect they deserve in Hollywood today and that one of the only ways he knows to maintain artistic control of a film is to keep the budget low.

And if you're writing a script and you get stuck inexorably in the maw of an epic case of writer's block, move into a cheap motel for a while and you'll be fine.

When you started this script, I read that you got terribly stuck at about thirty pages. Your brother then encouraged you to finish it, so you rented a cheap motel room off the 101 freeway where it turned out the desk clerk was at the Ambassador rally the night Bobby Kennedy was killed?

It's absolutely true. Her name was Dianne. I interviewed her three times during the three weeks that I stayed there. She had married two young men to keep them from going to Vietnam. She had spent that day canvassing out in Glendale and Pasadena and was in the ballroom for the victory speech. She heard the shots and said it was as if the rug had been pulled out from underneath an entire generation. I think that's a pretty accurate description of what happened after that night.

And after the motel, you were no longer blocked?

No, the writer's block was over.

INTERVIEWER
In the film, you tell the story of
Bobby Kennedy's assassination
through those around him rather
than by focusing on him. Why did
you use that construct?

EMILIO ESTEVEZ
I didn't want to make a straight
political biopic. To me it was about
ordinary people living their lives and
not knowing what lay ahead. These
are all people who had seats on the
Titanic; we all know the iceberg is
coming. This is an ordinary day,
these are ordinary people, and they
will soon find themselves at the epicenter of one of the most important
events of the twentieth century.

So you used the known conclusion of that day to establish a looming narrative tension?

Exactly. It's the elephant in the room and it [also] puts in perspective all the petty stuff that we get caught up in—the minutia of life we busy ourselves with. It plays on things like Helen Hunt's character talking about her shoes and how silly that is because, ultimately, later on in the film, she finds herself on the floor of the pantry with a bullet in her head.

Once I started researching the assassination, I discovered that there were five other people shot that day, so the randomness of violence is something else I wanted to explore. It's the idea that the bullet doesn't discriminate—rich or poor, famous or unknown.

You mentioned earlier that you finished this script for *Bobby* shortly before 9/11—how long exactly?

A couple of weeks. So here I am writing a story about ordinary people and a national tragedy and 9/11 happens and we go to war, you know? And now, years later, the immigration issue has become topical as well. This story has more relevance now than when I first wrote it. It looks oddly prophetic from that point of view.

You've been an actor, director, and screenwriter. Where do you rank screenwriting in terms of difficulty?

It's perhaps the most difficult and lonely of the three jobs, because, there you are . . .

In a cheap hotel room.

Right, and you've gotta come up with something. I'll tell you that I don't really like writing but I also love writing. I've been writing my whole life—short stories and poetry—going back to age seven. I submitted a story to Rod Serling's *Night Gallery* on lined notebook paper in like 1972. To have the audacity to do that is pretty hilarious.

Did he use it?

God, no!

When you worked with James Duff on the script adaptation for *The War at Home,* you put a lot into it and I've read you were disappointed with the performance of the film. Did you take any lessons from that experience?

I was not disappointed with how the movie turned out—I'm still proud of it. I was disappointed in how dismissed it was by the studio for whom I'd made a tremendous amount of money. I wished that it had enjoyed a longer theatrical life—it was released on like three screens.

That was not your idea of a "going wide"?

No. And we received a lot of terrific reviews, so for me it was really puzzling as to why the studio discarded it.

Have you gleaned any lasting lessons from that experience or is it just sort of a head scratcher?

It was a bit of a head scratcher. I think that writers today don't enjoy the same celebration in Hollywood that they enjoyed in the fifties. They're oftentimes disregarded. The same thing has happened a bit with directors, like we're this nuisance getting in the way of the studios. I'm not really sure why that is.

Do you see that situation turning around at all in the case of some of the young auteurs, films like *Adaptation*?

I only see it turning around if we can figure out how to make films more cheaply. If you're making movies that cost $100 million, the studio has you by the balls. They're paying you a lot of money, and they have stockholders to answer to. From a business perspective, that makes a lot of sense.

Of course you're not gonna let the lunatics run the asylum. But if we can get off that treadmill and make movies for $10 [million] and under, $20 [million] and under—movies where the return on investment makes a lot of sense, then perhaps we'll see a change. But not in the current state of things.

GEOFFREY FLETCHER

CAREER HIGHLIGHTS:
Precious; Violet & Daisy

"Looking back on all the time I felt like an outsider with an uncertain future . . . I wouldn't trade those difficult days for anything, because those experiences make one a better storyteller. They add depth, dimension, and truth to one's work."

—GEOFFREY FLETCHER

Geoffrey Fletcher went to the best schools: Harvard and then NYU Film. But the writer-director says his own despair on the outside of life is what most equipped him to adapt *Precious*, from the novel *Push* by Sapphire. After more than a decade of toiling fruitlessly as a writer and filmmaker, this was his first produced script and it won him an Oscar for best-adapted screenplay.

Fletcher was raised in an upper-middle-class home in Connecticut and went to tony prep schools worlds away from the brutally abused inner-city title-character at the film's center. But Fletcher discovered a connection with Precious through the parts of her he could feel deeply—her anguish feeling stuck on the outside of life as well as her dauntless dreaming.

Here Fletcher opens up about how close to despair he was when *Precious* came along. He also explains that in screenwriting, the heavy lifting of a piece is in the preparation, in this case with the original text, taking extensive notes and letting it work through the subconscious. And though he always tries to write during "normal" working hours, when he gets going, he inevitably winds up, as he did with *Precious*, writing through the wee hours until sunrise.

Tell me how you came to this project.

Lee Daniels saw a short film I'd written, shot, directed, and edited and was really taken by it, and he asked if I would get involved in this project. I had never heard of the book. I'm both grateful and embarrassed to admit that. I'm embarrassed because it's such a great work of art with a great following. I'm grateful because that might have intimidated or affected me in some way and inhibited my freedom in adapting it.

So, in a way, your ignorance of the book allowed you to come to this material clean and fresh?

Exactly. I came to it fresh and without any preconceptions or fear of changing things. I think it would have inhibited to some degree the freedom with which I felt I could approach it.

How shortly after your first read of this novel were you into the adaptation?

Immediately. And all throughout the reading of the book, I was writing extensive notes in the margins, in the back of the book, and in a separate file of notes. Throughout the first reading, I feel like my unconscious was organizing it, so much so that when I sat down to write, it came out fairly polished early on because of all the thinking that went on before the writing started.

I think all writing is difficult, but for me, thinking about what I'm going to write is the heavy lifting. The actual typing of the pages becomes much easier.

This material is so brutal, tragic, and visceral and yet it's hopeful. How do you think Sapphire struck that tone, and how did you preserve that in the script?

People told me that they cried for weeks after reading the book, and I was warned how heavy it was. I didn't experience that when I read it. I saw it as this beautiful journey. I thought it was so full of love and hope. I know that it goes to some grim places, but my filter and the prism through which I viewed it was very different.

The idea of making it accessible but being true to the novel's spirit was one of my goals. With cinema you can communicate a great deal—without necessarily showing everything, you can communicate everything. Which is what a lot of the great old horror films did—they let you scare yourself, they let you participate. So we didn't shy away from some of the more graphic areas, but we indicated them enough that the viewer could participate.

How long was it from the time you started reading _Precious_ to your first completed draft?

A few weeks of intense reading, thinking, and notes and roughly five months to a fairly polished draft.

INTERVIEWER
And on a practical level, what was
that five months like? Were you writing every day, the mornings, a few
days a week?

GEOFFREY FLETCHER
It ranged between five and six days
a week. It would start in what most
people consider normal working
hours. Whenever I write, invariably,
it shifts to very late at night, sometimes between the hours of midnight
and sunrise. The world outside is so
quiet then and the darkness sort of
wraps around you in this very nice
way. You can get into a very special
space with your thoughts and the
world within which you're working.
I saw a number of sunrises throughout the writing process.

Did this material take an emotional toll, just the process, having those quiet deep hours with this material and this world? Did it affect you outside of the writing?

It definitely did. I've been trying for so long to find a way into the industry. Filmmaking is the love of my life, and I feared I might never get the opportunity to express myself or make a living at it. Feeling outside for so long and really starting to wonder if I'd ever get a film made, there were times, particularly right before I got this job, that I'd begun to lose hope.

Writing this restored a sense of fulfillment, purpose, and contentment.

This was your dream shot?

Yes.

A resurrection?

That's an excellent word to describe it. I really did feel as if I'd come back from the dead.

Do you feel as though you maybe grafted your own personal emotional journey onto that of *Precious*?

These are excellent questions. I mean, really. Precisely. There are a number of specific experiences or theories or things that I've studied that worked their way into

Precious. Feeling on the outside and feeling like you have something to offer on the inside that other people may or may not see: I can relate to those feelings so strongly. I think it's partly why I related to *Precious* so strongly and made sure to use those experiences.

Looking back on all the time I felt like an outsider with an uncertain future—I mean, I don't think anyone has a certain future in this industry or isn't always hustling to see what's next—but I wouldn't trade those difficult days for anything, because those experiences make one a better storyteller. They add depth, dimension, and truth to one's work.

VINCE
GILLIGAN

CAREER HIGHLIGHTS:

Breaking Bad; *Hancock*; *The X-Files*

"With *Breaking Bad* I feel like I pulled the lever at the slot machine and it came up cherries. If it was something I did, I don't know if I could repeat it."

—VINCE GILLIGAN

Vince Gilligan turned a bitch session about writing in Hollywood into AMC's hugely successful show *Breaking Bad.* Kvetching with a writer buddy about not being able to land a good gig, he joked that he should start cooking meth out of the back of an RV.

And that's how you think up a hit show.

First and foremost, he says, "Keep swinging," and never give up. Beyond that, Gilligan has learned how an idea will grow beyond your wildest imagination with great collaborators, that you should never plot a script from a place of fear and, most importantly, never think about whether or not an idea will sell. If he'd done that, *Breaking Bad* never would have happened.

I've read that the seed for this show came out of kind of a bitch session with a buddy of yours about the TV business. Is that the power of negative thinking or *The Secret* in reverse or what?

I'd love to say I have a secret, but I don't. I think the only secret is a pretty open secret, that is to just keep swinging and not give up. It's ironic and amusing to me that *Breaking Bad* came out of a bitch session, as you say; bitching about how work was scarce and the good jobs were not that easy to find. That magic idea can come at any time. Sometimes you know it right away and other times you don't know it until later. It happened to come for me in the middle of a gripe-fest about my lack of employment.

It could have come at a high point or a low point. The secret is to just remain open to new ideas and not give up when they get turned down. *Breaking Bad* was turned down all over town before AMC finally bought it. That is not, as we all know, a remotely unusual story.

Did you know when you had this idea that it was a big one, or was it like others?

About five or six years ago I was talking to a buddy of mine, Tom Schnauz, who I attended NYU film school with. He and I had been on *The X-Files* as writers up until 2002. So this was probably three years after that show had ended. Pickings were slim.

Both of us had been unemployed for a while and we were wondering what to do next. Either he or I joked about putting a crystal meth lab in the back of an RV and driving around the country cooking meth and making money.

As we were talking, the idea for this character just kinda popped into my head. It was that proverbial lightning strike. It felt unusual because that doesn't happen for me. My ideas tend to come in much smaller pieces, and it's more work pulling it out and turning it into something usable.

I had this full-fledged character, this good, law-abiding man who suddenly decides to become a criminal. I was so intrigued by the character that I didn't really give much thought to how well it would sell, which is good because *Breaking Bad* is such an odd, dark story, it's not easily sold. If I'd spent too much time thinking about how tough it was going to be to sell, I might have psyched myself out of even trying.

INTERVIEWER
Has the resonance of this premise
and where it has led surprised you
once you really started developing
the story?

VINCE GILLIGAN
That's a good question. Yes, I would
say this concept and this show has
had legs beyond what I ever would
have imagined when I first came
up with the idea. I was thinking of
strictly this main character, this Walter White character. The idea of a
Walter Mitty kind of milquetoast character who reinvents himself and turns
from somebody good to somebody bad
and profits in the process. That was
the sum total of the concept.

As the show has gone to air and now
as we've shot thirty-three episodes
of the show, the richness of the other
characters and the aspects of this
world that we're able to comment on
are all things that are new and surprising to me.

They also show what a group effort
television really is. So much of the
show that is great and that I'm proud
of is stuff that I didn't see coming
and stuff that's not even my creation.

I've got seven other really talented
writers here who add immensely
to the show. And I've got a wonderful ensemble cast. It's immeasurable
what they've added to this show.
These characters exist because of
the writing and because of the acting
and it's hard to separate and mea-
sure which is the bigger contribution.
A similar thing could be said about
the directing too.

Can you give me a specific example of a theme or a tone that has emanated from this show that you didn't anticipate?

> Well, I guess it's tried and true, but I didn't realize how much family would play into the show. The idea of family being the bedrock of a person's existence and as something to be nurtured but also something that's easily destroyed. There's not a reinvention of the wheel in telling a story about family but I think we come back to it as writers so often because it's so important to all of us as individuals. I guess I didn't see that coming when I set out to do this.

The writers' strike actually helped you by delaying the last two episodes of the first season?

> It really did, it's true.

So before the strike, you didn't know if the show would stick and you kinda went with pretty sensational stuff in the last two episodes of that first season, hoping to grab what attention you could. But the strike gave you a pause to see how the show was gaining traction, and you were able to dial it back and take a slower, deeper arc with these characters. What did that teach you about how to balance the pressure of the business with your creative intent and instincts?

> There's an old joke I love about the old bull and the young bull. They're standing up on a hill looking out

over a pasture of cows and the young bull says "I'm gonna run down there and have sex with a cow," and the old bull says, "I'm gonna walk down there and have sex with all of them."

I'm trying to word it a little less crudely than usual.

It's weird because, I've heard that joke and it almost sounds more gross when you don't use the "f-word."

I guess it does, that's true. I guess I learned and am in the process of learning that less is more and oftentimes it's a benefit when you don't throw the kitchen sink at it.

Out of fear or . . .

Exactly. Especially that you don't make any of your plotting decisions out of fear or desperation. That is an important lesson for anyone to learn: to keep to the simple story and the characters rather than letting it all get away from you in an effort to please what is perceived to be an increasingly attention-deprived audience.

The show's either gonna work for you or not. The odds tell you it won't. Most shows don't work. And when they do work, it's kind of like winning the lottery. With *Breaking Bad* I feel like I pulled the lever at the slot machine and it came up cherries. If it was something I did, I don't know if I could repeat it.

Having said that, in hindsight, my good fortune was that I didn't have the opportunity to go with my first instincts and throw the kitchen sink plot-wise into our first season. If I'd done that I would have painted myself into some seriously unpleasant plot corners.

My general philosophy now more than ever is to give the audience the least possible—which sounds like a weird philosophy, but you want to parcel things out as slowly as you can. Of course what that means is, you want to parcel things out as slowly as you can while keeping things gripping and interesting.

I don't necessarily believe the conventional wisdom that the audience is always restless and more restless than ever and always needs more stimulation. People still like storytelling that can slow down enough to explore characters and examine them closely. I think there's still room for that. Hopefully that never gets lost completely.

GARRISON KEILLOR

CAREER HIGHLIGHTS:

A Prairie Home Companion; *The Sandy Bottom Orchestra*;
A Christmas Blizzard

"I'm not a major movie fan. I was brought up fundamentalist and so I associate filmdom with moral squalor and eternal damnation."

—GARRISON KEILLOR

Garrison Keillor has been treading the imaginary lanes and thought-up sidewalks of Lake Wobegon, bringing its homespun menagerie of local residents to life for the better part of four decades. He's written nearly his whole life: novels, radio plays, and endless columns syndicated all around the real world.

But he'd never written a screenplay until Robert Altman helped bring *A Prairie Home Companion* to the big screen in 2006. The aridly funny, endlessly self-deprecating Keillor says it was about the hardest thing he's ever had to write. Despite personifying a simpler, slower time, he readily admits he loves his laptop and uses it constantly to write everywhere—in hotels, airports, and even taxis.

This film represents your first screenplay credit. Did any functional surprises emerge during the process of translating *A Prairie Home Companion* to screenplay form?

Mr. Altman was very accommodating and congenial. He doesn't care for long meetings at which people sit and show off, so I got to sit home and just write the thing. And then, once he started shooting, he very kindly let me hang around and revise parts of it at the last minute. He's an improviser himself and so he gives the actors a certain license, and the writer as well, as it turned out.

That was a boon. Like playing golf and getting to improve your lie. The surprise is how complicated everything is. It takes fifty people several hours to film a belch. It's a miracle that any good movies get made.

Tell me a bit about your process working with writer Ken LaZebnik.

Ken wrote for the radio show years ago in New York, then he emigrated to L.A. and went into TV. He consulted on the development of the script, read each draft, and made comments, and he was a good sounding board. Plus which, he was very enthusiastic, which I'm not.

INTERVIEWER
As a storyteller, are there any
unique challenges to the medium of
film and screenwriting that you have
to surmount to get the same kind of
intimate character and story detail
that you achieve on the radio show?

GARRISON KEILLOR
Radio is a magical medium, and
movies are very hard work. Radio
employs language to the fullest. It
addresses mature people with some
experience in the world, which they
bring to the game, so a few references can produce images more vivid
than most of what you'd see on a
screen. You can do a monologue on
several different levels and the audience picks up everything and adds
their own experience and comes
away delighted.

A few times, during this picture, I
thought to myself, "I should've tried
this as a radio drama." But movies have the oomph of money and
sex appeal. Movie stars are the last
true celebrities in America. The challenge of movies for me is that I know
almost nothing about them.

I'm not a major movie fan. I was
brought up fundamentalist and so I
associate filmdom with moral squalor
and eternal damnation.

When you write, how and when do you do it? What's your ideal routine?

The laptop is a dreamy machine that enables you to take everything with you anywhere. So I write in hotel rooms, on airplanes, even in taxis. I like to write early in the morning. That's when the hard problems get worked out.

You said in a recent *San Francisco Chronicle* piece that you think you now want to be a playwright, as the literary world is too cold and you enjoy the social aspects of theater. You said this also applied to film. Do you see yourself doing more work as a screenwriter?

I have one more screenplay in me. I'll write that and then I'd love to direct it, if possible. That would round out my movie career. I am getting too old to be on public view, so I need to figure out a way to write the stuff and have it performed by other people. Performing is for twenty-year-olds. I'm old and jowly and have enormous eyebrows and my feet hurt.

STEVE
KLOVES

CAREER HIGHLIGHTS:

Harry Potter (seven of the franchise's eight films); *Wonder Boys*; *Racing with the Moon*

"I was always baffled early in my career in meetings with executives [who] would always ask, 'What's the first act curtain?' I always had to ask for edification because I didn't know what they were talking about."

—STEVE KLOVES

If you'd asked writer Steve Kloves at the turn of the millennium about a boy wizard called Harry Potter, he would have replied, "Harry who?"

At the time he was fresh from the triumph of his Academy Award–nominated script for *Wonder Boys*. Boy wizards were the furthest thing from his mind when yet another package in the deluge of scripts arrived for him to ignore.

"I honestly almost never read coverage of novels because it's usually such an impossible thing to do well," he says. "For some reason I opened this particular package of seven coverages and leafed through. I'm reading and I'm not interested, not interested, I *know* I'm not interested and then the seventh one is called *Harry Potter and the Philosopher's Stone* [the first book's United Kingdom title]." Something about the page-and-a-half synopsis bestirred his interest enough that he walked across the street to a bookstore and bought the book.

Though his prior work on films like *The Fabulous Baker Boys* and *Flesh and Bone* didn't readily appear an apt preparation for a children's book about spells and magic, Kloves says it made perfect sense to him when he read the first book.

"It never felt odd to me because all of my [prior work] had to do with dysfunctional families, kids who have been damaged, and damaged people. To me, Harry is the ultimate damaged character . . . right down to his scar."

He eventually wrote seven of the eight films (he took a self-imposed break on the fifth film, *Order of the Phoenix*). It became the highest-grossing film franchise in history. Here, in discussing *Harry Potter and the Goblet of Fire*, he explains how he prefers to follow the rhythm or music of a script rather than the structure.

And though you'd think he'd have developed some formulas after writing seven installments of one franchise, he insists there are no recipes in screenwriting. Every script is different.

You've done four *Harry Potter* scripts now. Have you developed a recipe for adapting these books, or is each one like starting from scratch?

There's no recipe. Anyone who's seen the movies can see that I have no recipe [*laughs*]. *Philosopher's Stone* was challenging in the sense that the actual plot came very late in the book, and it was all about setting up the world. The challenge of the most recent film, *Goblet of Fire,* was that it's too enormous a book for one movie.

Yeah, it's a big book and a great one.

Yeah, I love this book. It's my favorite *Harry Potter* book. The problem was justifying it being two movies. Warner Brothers didn't have the appetite for two, and I can understand why, because the book doesn't actually lend itself to being two full movies; it's more like a movie-and-a-half or a movie-and-three-quarters.

They've all been challenging in different ways. Jo's [author J. K. Rowling] plots are fiendish. I used to joke that the one element, if there is a recipe to her plots, is that there's always the "Dumbledore explains it all" scene. In the books, that's kind of the way it works because you don't know what's going on and then Dumbledore tells you. If it wasn't Dumbledore in the books, it often is in the movies—Dumbledore or Hermione, who carries exposition really well.

She's your favorite character, I understand?

Yeah, I always loved Hermione because I thought she was the kind of girl that would have driven me crazy in school and that I would have been desperately in love with. So smart and funny.

Having written a lot of adult, dialogue-driven films like *Baker Boys*, do you feel handcuffed in terms of dialogue when dealing with children's fantasy?

I'd be lying if I said I didn't feel somewhat handcuffed, but only because the demands of the movies make it so there's so much to stuff in, and you only have so much room. On the other hand, dialogue is my favorite thing to do, and I like these characters very much, so it's enormously challenging. There's so much to play with in their interaction.

But I feel hamstrung in every film that way. In *Baker Boys* there's a seven-minute balcony scene. I'm one of those writers who likes to write scenes that are almost mini-movies, [and] that's just not going to happen with *Harry Potter*. They're not going to let me write a seven-minute dialogue scene. I've done it a couple times, but it inevitably gets trimmed back. It's not just *Harry Potter*; most of the directors I've worked with are like, "What the hell are you doing?" I think the reason I was allowed to do it in *Baker Boys* was because I was directing it and I was all for it.

Are structure and pacing the key challenges when it comes to scripting a *Harry Potter* book?

I'm not the greatest guy when it comes to structure. It would be a lie for me to say I was. I see movies in terms of rhythm more than structure. I see movies like music; going from one scene to another and the rhythm of each scene. I was always baffled early in my career in meetings with executives [who] would always ask, "What's the first act curtain?" I always had to ask for edification because I didn't know what they were talking about.

To me, if you're gonna break it down, my first-act curtain might be on page fifteen, never on page thirty-five. I don't see movies like plays; I see them in a whole different way. I think that's because the movies that I cut my teeth on and was inspired by were the movies of the late sixties and seventies, which were often kind of meandering and went down blind alleys only to emerge in a more interesting place.

More like jazz?

It's true, more like jazz. I mean, it sounds pretentious but I've always seen movies that way. A friend of mine said, "What you do well is riffing and if you're too constrained, it kinda doesn't work sometimes."

There was this kind of tension on *Goblet of Fire*, between [director] Mike Newell and me. I think it became a really good partnership because he was intent on making it a thriller. Mike is very smart about structure and those kinds of things. I was intent on playing out the social comedy of these kids suddenly crashing into puberty. So it was two forces willing our visions into the piece, and I think we ended up with a combination that is pleasing.

We got along great because Mike is so humane and such a great guy that he was always tickled by the social comedy. It's not that he didn't want to embrace it, he just wanted it to have an engine and that was the thriller element, and he really brought that to *Goblet of Fire*.

INTERVIEWER
What do you think is most distinctive
about this installment in the saga?

STEVE KLOVES
For me it's social comedy. Puberty
is an odd word for it. It's a line that
I wrote that they're using for the
tag line for the ad: "Everything will
change now." For me what it's about
is the fact that nothing will be the
same at the end of this movie. It's
a real curtain. The series is a completely different beast after this.

ELMORE
LEONARD

CAREER HIGHLIGHTS:
Get Shorty (novel adapted to film); Out of Sight (novel adapted to film); Rum Punch (adapted by Quentin Tarantino into Jackie Brown); 3:10 to Yuma (short story adapted into two features)

"There was a time when I had to [write scripts for studios] 'cuz I needed the money. I wasn't very proud of the pictures, but it was just something I had to do. There was no way to talk [executives] into anything. You'd have a story conference on a Friday afternoon and they'd give you all this stuff, all their ideas. You'd go back to your hotel room, sit there looking at the wall and writing it, and then Monday you'd meet 'em again, and they'd forgotten all the bullshit they'd told you Friday."

—ELMORE LEONARD

Elmore Leonard is essentially always writing. As engaging a conversationalist as he is, as keen and sincere a listener, he is always a little bit somewhere else, playing with the menagerie of characters he's created over his prolific six-decade career. He just strolls effortlessly, like a Jazz Age tap dancer, between the world that is real—where you are—and the dozens of places he's created over the years, first in longhand and then on a Selectric electric typewriter.

Hollywood has always liked Leonard, even if he's had some trouble with it. His first adaptation of the short story "3:10 to Yuma" (which he originally sold to Dime Western Magazine for ninety bucks) hit theaters in 1957 and starred Glenn Ford. Leonard says he's struggled with screenwriting, which he doesn't feel he's very good at.

Still he's enjoyed great success as others adapt his work: from *Get Shorty* and *Out of Sight* (both from screenplays by Scott Frank) to Quentin Tarantino's *Jackie Brown*, based on his novel *Rum Punch*. He's easily one of the top five most adapted pulp authors in the history of film, and that's counting the likes of Agatha Christie and James M. Cain.

During an expansive chat about his small screen hit *Justified* (the FX series inspired by his recurring character, U.S. Marshal Ray-lan Givens), he gives a master class in simple, well-burnished truths of writing.

Among them:

- Research is crucial because the truth is always more interesting.
- Don't plan bits of your story in advance, because you won't like 'em when you actually get there.
- Audition your characters at the beginning of a story to find out which ones you really want to develop.
- Focus on good stories instead of money and the money will come.
- Don't ever use words your characters don't know.

You've had good and bad experiences with your work being adapted. What are your feelings about what's being done with *Justified*?

I love it. I think they've got my sound down and they're running with it. Did you hear about the little bracelets they wear?

No, I didn't.

They're rubber and on them, I think it's kind of raised lettering, is written "W.W.E.D.?"—"What Would Elmore Do?" They're trying to stay in my mind, you know, and write offbeat lines and hard lines and do what I do. I think it's great.

Apparently the bracelets are working.

I think so.

They used *Fire in the Hole* as the pilot, and they're using parts from a couple of other books that Raylan Givens is in. They're not [direct adaptations] though, because they fool with it and set it up in a different way, but it works.

[Givens] was in *Pronto* and *Riding the Rap* . . . There's a girl in *Riding the Rap* who's in another book, the last book [*Road Dogs*], Dawn Navarro. I wanted to keep her out of it, at least for the time being because I might do another book with her.

You keep all these characters alive in a kind of constellation in your mind, don't you?

Yeah, sure. I finish a book and wonder what they're doing now. Like they're mannequins left in some position, waiting to be moved.

When you started writing Westerns, you discovered early the importance of presenting the real details from the lives of cowboys and Indians, rather than the TV stereotypes out at the time. You really set to researching New Mexico, Arizona, American Indian history . . .

The kind of guns they used, the clothes, yeah. I researched Apaches primarily and cowboys, cowboys and cavalry for the most part in Arizona. There was a lot of stuff written about them at the time. There were serials in the *Saturday Evening Post* and *Collier's* about the cavalry fighting the Apaches.

I liked the Apaches. I thought they were really bad. They didn't wear feathers, they just had long hair and a band around their head. I liked that.

Not your typical TV Indian.

All the TV [Westerns], at least for the first year, ended with a gunfight in the street. I read in the research that that would rarely ever happen. If you wanted to shoot someone, you just walk into the saloon and shoot 'em, you know?

So it's a case of the truth being more interesting?

Yes, definitely.

You tend to start off a new book with a character and a basic situation and then just go from there without any outline or notion of the end. What do you think that approach has given your writing that a more preplanned approach would not?

I found early on that when you think of a scene that you might subsequently use, when you finally get to the point of using it, you're kind of stuck with it. Then you think about it again and you say, "Well, geez, I'm not doing this right. It could be a lot more fun and interesting."

When the ideas occur as you're writing, as you're going along, it just works better. You don't have to belabor some idea that you had a couple months before.

INTERVIEWER

But what do you do then when you're stumped, when you're cold in the moment? I don't know, maybe you don't get stumped.

ELMORE LEONARD

No, I do. I'll think of a way to do the scene that will lead me out of it and leave me a way to not have to explain what's in the guy's mind at this particular moment. That's when I'm usually stopped, when I'm asking, "Okay, what's his attitude right now?"

The best thing to do is get away from that. Maybe he imagines a conversation with somebody where he describes his problem.

[But usually] within the first 100 pages I know who my characters are. Then there's always a new character who'll slip in later on, and I'll say, "Oh God, I've gotta give him a name. I like this guy; he's important."

Then something else happens in the story, a subplot maybe.

So they just come and prove to you what their voice is?

Yeah. They're kind of auditioned in the first scenes that
they appear in. [For example], a guy owns a casino hotel,
and he's got a lot of money, and I think he's one of the
main characters. Then he talks to a guy that he hired to
run all the gambling action in the casino. The first time
the two of them are together, I see that I like this guy,
Jackie Garbo [from 1985's *Glitz*], better than the guy who
owns the casino. So he's kind of pushed off.

The point being, you cannot limit yourself by your plans?

That's the idea, right.

Has writing gotten harder or easier over all these years?

It's gotten a little harder. It takes me longer. It could
be my age, too, but it took me a year to write my latest
book, *Djibouti* [which centers on East African pirates
and Al Qaeda]. I had more research and more studying
to do, with the help of my researcher [Gregg Sutter]. I
couldn't see my desk for almost a year. But it was worth
it because I like the book.

You've said that you've approached writing both with a desire to write and to make as much money doing it as you can. Do you think that kind of honest, unpretentious attitude toward writing has helped you be a better, more productive writer?

Oh, definitely. All writers are in it for the money. What other reason is there?

But what about the notion of the starving artist, not selling out?

Samuel Johnson once said that anyone who would not write for money is a fool. You know? From the horse's mouth! That's why we're doing it but still attempting to do it as well as we can and not sacrifice our voice. I'm not going to write like some guy who's making a lot more money than I am just because he is.

Frankly, it's not that important. The story is the important thing and then go for the money.

Are there any perils to writing with money in mind?

I'm not writing with money in mind. I'm making the writing as good as I can. I'm at my limit. I can't do it any better. Every once in a while I'll think I can and I'll try a different thing, but I'm at my limit.

You've also said that screenwriting is work to you because you feel like an employee. Is there any aspect of it that has taught you something about writing in general, or is it just a chore?

It was a chore [mostly] because you've got several bosses. You're not just writing for yourself. I write for myself. I'm the only one I have to please. When I have to please a producer and a director and so on, then I'm just taking in writing, doing what they want me to do.

There was a time when I had to do it, 'cuz I needed the money. I wasn't very proud of the pictures, but it was just something I had to do. There was no way to talk [executives] into anything. You'd have a story conference on a Friday afternoon, and they'd give all this stuff, all their ideas, [and] you'd go back to your hotel room, sit there looking at the wall and writing it, and then Monday you'd meet 'em again, and they'd forgotten all the bullshit they'd told you Friday.

Your golden rule of writing has been to write in a way that does not feel like writing. Do you have any additions to that philosophy, and do you feel it applies to screenwriting?

I don't know. That's something I did have trouble with when screenwriting because when I'm writing a scene, it's always from a character's point of view; it's how he reacts to what's happening. The other people in the scene will tell him all sorts of things, but it's him and his mind that's driving the scene.

That's the way I write. I can switch viewpoints as well to characters I like or who have something to say, but I'm never in it. I don't use any words that might be more appropriate if I were writing as a literary writer. I don't use any words that my characters don't know. I wanna keep that sound, their sound.

How much of your mental time and energy is consumed by thinking about these characters and these stories?

Once I know who my characters are, I see them all the time. I'm with them all the time. I quit work at six o'clock. I take a shower and try to forget 'em, but I don't.

You can't?

No, I can't.

Does it ever get maddening?

Well, my wife will say, "God! Who are you now?" I never use their language, but she will see an attitude that isn't mine.

RICHARD LINKLATER

CAREER HIGHLIGHTS:

Fast Food Nation; *Dazed and Confused*; *Slacker*

"I like story and characters. Plot is kind of a trickier thing for me. I'm not that imaginative, I guess, with plot twists and turns. I don't think that way because I don't think life unfolds that way very often."

—RICHARD LINKLATER

Richard Linklater is not sure why he often gets categorized with stoner filmmakers despite rarely referencing pot or drugs in his films. The writer-director became an indie darling with his lovably rudderless 1991 film *Slacker*—a film often credited with birthing that quintessential '90s meme.

In a conversation about his rotoscoped film *A Scanner Darkly*, which he adapted from a Philip K. Dick story, he says plotting has never been his thing.

Still, as unstructured as his plots tend to be, his approach to writing has become very disciplined and "craftsman like." When he's working on a script, he works every day. If he's stuck in one area—say dialogue—he works on descriptions or something else but never quits. Maybe it's this discipline or just getting older, but he says the writer's block that plagued him in his twenties is long gone.

To what extent did *A Scanner Darkly* appeal to you as kind of a cautionary response to your earlier films like *Slacker* and *Dazed and Confused*?

I don't really relate it to those films at all, but it was definitely something that interested me. The film is a cautionary tale about drug use and self-medicating. *Slacker* doesn't really have any drug use but people think it's kind of a trippy movie.

Somehow I've gotten to be known as this drug filmmaker while rarely referencing drugs. *Dazed* is kind of a pot-party movie. *Scanner* is much more serious. The drug depicted in the book, called Substance D, is much more sinister and dangerous.

I'm not trying to say all your movies are drug movies.

No, a lot of 'em are, believe me.

It's just that, the sobriety and darkness of this film's message seems a departure for you tonally. What appealed to you about it?

I don't know. You can't help but respond to the world around you a little bit. Maybe it's getting a little older. It's a pretty sober view of the idea that, if you're going to play, there's a dark side to it. There's kind of a sinister side to the world . . . it's pretty easy to be paranoid right now.

The book has a smaller national security aspect to it; mainly it focuses on a failed drug war. To what extent did you massage the adaptation to heighten it's correlation to what's going on today with domestic spying?

You couldn't help but see the parallel. It's interesting the way time has treated what Philip K. Dick wrote thirty years ago. He's become more prescient as we go. The book depicts a drug war before that term even existed. Set in the post-9/11 world, it seemed very much of our time.

It's easy to see how the drug war and the terror war will just all be part of the perpetual wars. It's kind of crazy the mess governments can put themselves and the individual in by declaring unwinnable wars on abstract things that are, in a way, natural offshoots of human behavior.

Many of your films have an unconventional approach to plot. Tell me briefly how you approach the plotting process with your own original scripts.

[*laughs*]

That's good. Your first response to the question is laughter.

I like story and characters. Plot is kind of a trickier thing for me. I can only take my cues from my life and the natural world around me. I'm not that imaginative, I guess, with plot twists and turns. I don't think that way

because I don't think life unfolds that way very often.
So I need help with that.

I'm glad in a situation like this, to have some of those
things inherent in the story. I mean, I appreciate plot as
much as the next guy, so *Scanner* for me is the best of
both worlds because it fits my own meandering narrative, but then it has some really wonderful plot twists
and turns I could have never come up with on my own
probably [*laughs*].

This is actually one of Dick's looser plots?

Yeah, very much.

And this is your first adaptation, right?

It's my first novel [adaptation]. I've done plays and
some stuff like that.

**So did the loose plot work to your advantage or make the
adaptation trickier?**

I read a lot of novels and don't ever think, "Hey, I could
make this into a movie." I read this and said, "Hey, I can
do this!" [*laughs*] It fit into my own world of storytelling
and character. I love Philip K. Dick so much, but this is
the one I felt chosen for. In my own self-deluded way I
was like, "That's mine to tell. I know that world, I know
those people, I can tell that story."

Was it daunting at all to take on such an oft-adapted, widely read author?

If you think about it too much, it can be kind of daunting, but I felt like I had the take. I felt like my instincts would probably be correct, you know? That I shared his view in imagining this world, so I didn't really think about it too much. It was kind of a matter of just bringing it out of the '70s, making the references more contemporary.

When and where do you do your writing?

I sit down and just do it. When I get in writing mode I just sit down for three to five hours every day. Sometimes I'll get on a roll and write all day or night. [But generally] I take a real craftsman-like approach. I don't wait around to be inspired; I just sit down and work.

I've found it easier and less emotionally volatile to just sit down and work. If the dialogue's not coming, work on something else like plotting or descriptions. Be easy on yourself. I think the blank page can be kind of intimidating. And maybe it's getting older too, I never really suffer writer's block. I can pretty much write anytime, anywhere.

INTERVIEWER
Did you used to suffer writer's block?

RICHARD LINKLATER
In my early twenties especially, I had
so much going on in my head and so
little patience to sit down and try to
write. I felt kind of overwhelmed. As
I got older, I got a little more patient
and easier on myself. It got a lot easier for me.

ALLAN
LOEB

CAREER HIGHLIGHTS:

Things We Lost in the Fire; *Wall Street: Money Never Sleeps*;
The Dilemma

"What kept me in it was laziness and fear. It would be nice to say it was passion and that I'm a struggling artist who didn't give up on his craft. All of that sounds good. But the truth is, it was laziness and fear."

—ALLAN LOEB

Allan Loeb is real-life screenwriter as Hollywood ending. He was a broke gambling addict who had toiled unsuccessfully for a decade trying to write a script he thought the market wanted. Then, the day his agent dumped him, he sat down and wrote the script *he'd* always wanted to write.

It was called *The Only Living Boy in New York* (the title comes from the Simon & Garfunkel tune) and it was a smash among Hollywood powerbrokers, vaulting him overnight from a washup to literally one of Hollywood's hottest scripters.

With a fistful of films and TV shows produced or in production, he talks straight about how—unlike nearly every writer on the planet—he loves almost everything he writes. He says he gets his freshest ideas during daily five-mile walks. Now that he's no longer gambling and success has arrived in spades, he adds, all he does other than walk, is write.

You kinda treaded water as a screenwriter for over a decade before writing *The Only Living Boy in New York*. What changed about your screenwriting approach to take you to the next level?

There were a few things. Quitting gambling really did help me redirect a lot of my energy toward writing. I was writing, but the gambling habit was very intense and draining.

The other thing was kind of an epiphany. I always really wanted to sell things. If I finished a spec script, I'd need to sell it to have any money. That was scary and often the focus. When the script didn't sell, the depression would kick in and so on.

So I kinda changed that paradigm and said, "Okay, I'm not gonna worry if this script sells or not." The goal is to make each script I write better than the last. If I feel like I'm getting better with each script, then I'll be okay. I held on to that, and it was kind of an epiphany in a way.

When you moved to New York in '04 and started writing *Living Boy*, your agent had just dropped you, right?

I got dropped by my agent literally the day I wrote "FADE IN" on *The Only Living Boy in New York*.

As you were writing "FADE IN," what did you think you would do if this last shot was a bust?

> I didn't know. I didn't know. Starting in about 2002, I knew for a fact that I had to get out of this business. It was too hard. It wasn't that I wasn't good enough, it was that it was too hard. What kept me in it was laziness and fear. It would be nice to say it was passion and I'm a struggling artist who didn't give up on his craft. All of that sounds good, but the truth is it was laziness and fear.

Wow.

> And I always say to people, I made the wrong decision, by the way. It worked out for me, but the right decision would have been to get out. All signs were telling me to get out and they were right at the time. I know that doesn't make sense, but it's true.

Do you have any doubts or anxieties now that you have been sucked back into the trade?

> No. It's weird. For the most part, 90 percent of what I do in my life I couldn't love any more. I love being a screenwriter; I love writing and getting paid to be doing what I'm doing. I feel like the luckiest person in the world. I know that sounds contradictory to what I just said, but it's not in a weird way.

At the time I should have gotten out. Nothing was happening, I was in my mid-thirties, I was broke, and you can't do that. You can't just stay with it. If it hadn't worked out, I don't know. When do you get out? At thirty-eight, it's much harder than at thirty-three and at forty-four it's much harder, and at fifty, what are you going to do? At some point, you have to walk away if it's not happening for you and I had passed that point. The only thing keeping me in was fear.

Because you didn't know what else to do?

I was too afraid to do what I should have done and what was needed and that was to make a move, to do something else, make some money, have a career that would pan out.

But since that point, you've penned and sold about a half dozen scripts. Have you simply been chained to your computer?

I work; I like to work a lot and on two or three things at a time. Since 2004, I've worked my ass off. That's all I do is write. I would say between television and film, I've worked on twelve or fourteen projects since '04.

At the peak of this frenzy of productivity, what's your day like?

> I have to do a lot away from the desk to keep the instrument sharp, if that makes sense. I exercise. I definitely have to walk. I walk five miles almost every day and that's where a lot of the good stuff comes.

Five miles a day?

> Yeah, I walk fast. It takes about an hour and twenty minutes. I put my iPod on, listen to my music, get my heart rate up a little bit and at the same time get into a trance-like state where all the good dialogue and good character stuff comes. That's where I'm doing my writing. Then when I'm sitting at the computer, I'm downloading that, so, sitting at the computer is not a painful process. It's essentially very quick. I can pound out six pages in an hour because I'm constantly ruminating on what those six pages will be during my daily life.

INTERVIEWER
Are you a streaky, up-and-down
writer or are you always pretty fast?

ALLAN LOEB
The business is up and down, the
responses are up and down, but I'm
pretty much always fast.

I'm the opposite of the perfectionist
writer who hates everything he does.
To tell you the truth, I love everything that I do. I'm married to my
shit the minute it comes off the key-
board and that's why it's always hard
to get notes; I'm always in love with
everything. I think that's very rare.

That's one of the famous perils of screenwriting, being too in love with your work.

But I think it really helps me. I think that people get paralyzed. Look, whether your stuff is good or not, if you love it, you're going to produce it and be prolific—you can write four or five scripts a year. If nothing is ever good enough, you're probably going to bang out a script every two or three years. And it still might not be good, by the way. It is a subjective art form.

So you can't create from a judgmental place?

Yeah and I don't for the most part. There's a lot of checks and balances out there. There's your friends, your agents, your producers, your studios executives, your directors—I've got a lot of people telling me why my shit sucks and then I can go make it better. Then it's easier to say, hey, it's good now. I'll leave that up to them.

So you've kind of grown to trust the universe out there?

Yeah, but the truth is, when it's good, they all love it. And that's so rare. I've been fortunate enough a few times—*Things We Lost in the Fire* was one of those times—where I get the script out, forty people read it, and forty people love it and it's just good. Most of the time, that's not the case.

DANNY MCBRIDE AND JODY HILL

CAREER HIGHLIGHTS:

Eastbound & Down; Your Highness; The Foot Fist Way

"We all just did what people do when they move to L.A.; try to get it going. Jody and I both worked at the Crocodile Cafe, we were both personal assistants on this show *Battle Dome,* you know, just trying to make it however we could. I still remember getting that job on *Battle Dome* like a week after we got out here [in 1999] and thinking, 'It's already happening for us! Let's do this shit!'"

—DANNY MCBRIDE

There's a voiceover in the debut season of Danny McBride and Jody Hill's juvenile and weirdly heart-warming HBO comedy *Eastbound & Down* that helps explain them and the show's success.

Balloon ego-ed Kenny Powers, the impenetrably mulleted, ex-major league pitcher at the series' center, realizes, after several epic humiliations, that he may actually be "just like everybody else, normal, not special, no hopes and dreams, pretending to be happy when he's really super sad."

Powers is always imagining himself as much more than he is and failing. Ever since Ralph Kramden on *The Honeymooners*, that basic narrative formula has been a hit.

McBride explains their approach much more simply: "We try to be really fuckin' funny."

He created the show with fellow N.C. (North Carolina) School of the Arts alums Ben Best and Jody Hill—the same pals with whom he made the micro-indie feature *Foot Fist Way*. *Foot* (which he also starred in) got the attention of comedy kingpins Will Ferrell and Adam McKay and scored McBride a streak of gut-busting cameos in films from *Pineapple Express* (directed by fellow N. C. School of the Arts alum David Gordon Green) to *Tropic Thunder* and *Up in the Air*. It also helped ultimately get *Eastbound* on TV.

McBride and Hill talk about *Eastbound & Down,* how the show, as redonkulous as it is, has roots in hard, autobiographical truth and why you don't need to like a hero if watching him struggle to realize his foolish dreams is funny.

And to all you moonlighting screenwriters out there, McBride says he's been there, and he feels your pain: Working on a screenplay after waiting tables for ten hours sucks.

Am I correct that you guys thought up this show while sitting in a baby pool drinking beers?

Danny McBride: That would be correct. Yes, that is the genesis of the show.

So it's a hot summer day, and you're in North Carolina at the time, right?

Danny McBride: That's correct. It was a hot day, and our buddy Chris Waldorf had a baby pool and, being grown men, we decided to get in that pool and we're not just gonna sit inside a shallow baby pool without drinking alcohol, so there was beer. As we started to prune, we started to get ideas for something to work on. That was the first time I think we ever talked about Kenny Powers, was in that meeting.

I love that you call that a meeting. So Kenny Powers is the show, this dude who returns to his hometown?

Danny McBride: Yes, basically. At the time a lot of us were facing that. I had just left Los Angeles and moved in with my parents and Ben [Best, the third buddy-co-creator], and Jody was back visiting; he hadn't fully surrendered to Los Angeles. We were all at this point in our lives where we'd left home with the greatest of intentions and things hadn't gone exactly as planned. We were all starting to face coming back home.

It wasn't like we had far to fall. We hadn't accomplished a damn thing. But I think it was that idea of coming back home after being away for a while, trying to rekindle those friendships that maybe you had neglected a little bit in your self-absorbed quest to make it.

As we started joking around about that we thought, wouldn't it be more fun if we had a guy who had a lot farther to fall than we had? And a guy who had kind of gone out of his way to burn some of those bridges? That's where he was born.

What year was this?

Jody Hill: This was 2002, I think?

Danny McBride: Yeah, I think so.

So pre–*Foot Fist Way*?

Jody Hill: Yes, definitely.

And you guys aren't really big sports fans either, right?

Danny McBride: I don't dislike sports, by any means. You know, I'm like a terrible athlete. I've been to games and have a fuckin' blast watchin' 'em. But I only have so much room in my head and in my personal life. It's always been used to memorize the names of bands and directors I like. That's always where my attention has been.

It's not that I dislike sports . . .

You're just not a rabid sports guy?

Danny McBride: Yeah, exactly.

Jody Hill: For me sports is the source of a lot of the insecurity and inadequacy that has followed me since I was about five years old into my adult life. I do not like sports. I do not follow sports, and I try to avoid any conversations that involve any knowledge of sports.

Well done on that front.

Jody Hill: Yeah, thank you.

You've started a hit show about a baseball player . . .

Jody Hill: A hit show and a movie about a karate guy.

If I can go back a bit, before making *Foot Fist Way* you guys toiled in L.A. for about seven years, right?

Jody Hill: That's about right.

Danny McBride: Yeah, we moved out there in '99 when we graduated school and came out with a group of buddies that we'd gone to school with. We all just did what people do when they move to L.A.: try to get it going. Jody and I both worked at the Crocodile Cafe, we were both personal assistants on this show *Battle Dome,* you know, just trying to make it however we could. I still remember getting that job on *Battle Dome* like a week after we got out here and thinking, "It's already happening for us! Let's do this shit!"

Oh man, so many people have had that *Battle Dome* experience. When you first came out and were all young and pumped and ready to rock, was the idea that you would be writers or directors?

Jody Hill: For me that was kind of the plan. I came out with a couple screenplays in hand and thought that I would try to sell those and that would be my way into the industry. It didn't work out that way.

What about you Danny?

Danny McBride: I had the same idea. I went to School of the Arts to be a director. That was my major there, and acting just came from being in each others' films. When I moved to L.A. I was focused on writing because I just figured that I'm not going to have the money to make a film right now, so I'll just write a screenplay that hopefully someone will read. I was just working in the days doing the P. A.-ing and waiting tables and then working on scripts at night, trying to get it together.

INTERVIEWER
How much writing did you guys
really do during those seven years?
Did you bang out a bunch of scripts
or struggle with a couple? Did a lot
of writing and learning go on during
those seven years?

DANNY MCBRIDE
I toiled on the same script for like
three years when I got out here
because you never really feel like
working on a screenplay after waiting tables and not being tipped for
ten hours a day, you know? So one
script took three years.

After *Foot Fist Way* I was finally
able to sell that script. It hasn't been
made or anything, but that was a
moment of victory that those three
years of toiling turned into a sale at
the end of the day. I think I mainly
focused on that. And I would gener-
ate a lot of ideas, start a lot of things
that I wouldn't finish. Those are the
same ideas that we kind of come
back to now that we're in a place to
actually have someone read our shit.

Is it weird that now people give a shit about your ideas after all those years?

> *Jody Hill*: To some degree it is. It's a very nice thing. Now it's become the type of thing where I don't wanna just sell every idea I have. I wanna make sure the choices are good in terms of the movies I want to make. It's just a different type of thing you think about now.
>
> But the idea of somebody who will volunteer to read your stuff? That's a luxury we have now.

Just out of curiosity, what was that script that you finally sold, Danny?

> *Danny McBride*: It was a movie called *Most Scariest* that was about a haunted frat house. It was like this fucked-up fraternity that moves into a haunted house and comedy and a few bumps in the night ensue.

Nice. And probably some boobs in there.

> *Danny McBride*: Yeah, there were a few boobs in there.

Haunted boobs.

> *Danny McBride*: Dead boobs and living boobs. Both.

When you guys began developing *Eastbound* in earnest, once you actually got into breaking story, did the material surprise you at all in terms of what it could do, like a car you don't really know until you start driving?

Jody Hill: One thing that actually made us want to take this from an idea to an actual developed show is the fact that Danny and I wanted to work together again in the same way we had on *Foot Fist Way,* where he's in front of the camera and I'm behind the camera and we're both in synch in terms of an anti-hero we both could explore over a long period of time. With *Foot Fist Way*, it was a short period of time. We both wanted to do something over a longer term.

Foot Fist Way was great because it prepared us for doing this kind of fucked-up humor about an unlikable guy. So I don't know if we were surprised. We were well aware of the goal we were aiming for in terms of tone and comedy and certainly we were both on the same page in terms of pushing each other as far as we could with that.

That makes sense about how *Foot Fist Way* prepared you for this kind of character and humor, but what about doing it in the long, episodic form?

Danny McBride: Honestly, I thought that the episodic format was the saving grace as far as reapproaching that sort of comedy. We had used a character like that in *Foot Fist Way* where he had to go on the arc of an hour-and-a-half movie . . . Another hour-and-a-half movie would have just felt like we were repeating ourselves.

With the episodic [format], we were able to take the arc of this guy and spread it out. We didn't have to make every story about pushing his character forward. We were able to slow it down and develop characters like Stevie and Cutler. That's where we started having a lot of fun was developing these other characters and the people that he lives with.

I think the biggest surprise is how people have responded to the material. With *Foot Fist Way* we were just making what we thought was funny and really had no concept or idea that anything would come of it. We had our fingers crossed, but, you know, it wasn't like that movie reached the masses by any means. We understood that working with that kind of material, we might always be limiting ourselves and our audience . . . So with *Eastbound*, we haven't pulled any punches but we've somehow found this audience that we couldn't find with *Fist*.

Maybe it's just the way Danny is on camera. How do you make Kenny Powers likable despite him being a ridiculously horrible person?

Jody Hill: I think Danny does have a lot to do with it, the fact that he's able to take this really unlikable character and infuse it with this humor and human quality. The other element is that Kenny Powers has dreams.

He has goals and vision. Traditional thinking is that he has to have a goal, but he also has to be likable, but I don't know if that's necessarily true. I think you're able to follow a guy if he has a goal and we believe that he believes in that.

Just to see him aspire?

Jody Hill: Exactly.

Danny McBride: And I think a lot of it comes down to what's entertaining to watch. It's a thirty-minute comedy. We're not trying to change the world or anything, we're just trying to tell a fucked-up story from a different point of view. So whether what he's doing is right or wrong, or morally corrupt, as long as it's entertaining at the end of the day, that gives you a lot of leeway with the audience.

It's not like we're trying to draw a thin line with Kenny Powers: "Is he a good guy or a bad guy?" It's pretty obvious that he's a bad dude. This is just a bad dude who's trying to fix himself and find redemption, like anyone who's normal. You're just watching his very fucked-up, hopefully entertaining, way to get there.

CHRISTOPHER AND JONATHAN NOLAN

CAREER HIGHLIGHTS:
The Dark Knight; Inception; Memento

"I don't ever think of screenwriting as separate components the way that studios sometimes like you to. I actually think of screenwriting as being one thing, so I don't think of it in terms of Jonathan being better at dialogue and me at story or something like that. We just throw the draft back and forth as a whole thing."
—CHRISTOPHER NOLAN

Though it in no way applies to their work, Christopher and Jonathan Nolan are kind of like a real-life, much-cooler version of *The Parent Trap* (the 1998 one with Lindsay Lohan). Both were born in the United Kingdom, but the elder, Christopher, was raised and schooled in the U.K., and the younger brother, Jonathan, grew up in the Chicagoland area. One speaks with a posh British accent, and the other sounds as American as a John Hughes film.

It's true, their father was a Brit and their mom a Yank, and Jonathan studied stateside while Chris went to a British university, but life is rarely like a Disney film. They are also not twins and, in actuality, Christopher spent a good amount of time growing up in Chicago, too.

Regardless, though they don't always work together (Chris directs and cowrites and Jonathan just cowrites), when they do, really fantastic things happen. From their breakthrough film, *Memento*, which was based on a story by Jonathan, through *The Dark Knight* and *The Dark Knight Rises,* they write exceptionally well together.

They speak here about the writing of their film *The Prestige* (which stars Christian Bale, Hugh Jackman, and Scarlett Johansson). They say their similar brains but disparate backgrounds are a huge advantage when writing, allowing them to expand the script's perspective. They also say that the security of brotherly trust is a powerful incubator of creative success.

This story, [*The Prestige*] based on the Christopher Priest novel, is not only period but it has a classic, old-school *Death-trap* kind of drama to its story. Was that one of the appeals?

Christopher Nolan: There is a very compelling old-fashioned appeal to the world of magic and the ideas of mystery and deception that it inspires. To me those are all very cinematic qualities, so I think that was my initial interest in the story.

Jonathan Nolan: Chris told me about the book on a long walk a number of years ago, even before I'd read it. He'd already broken it down . . . into the ideas that he was interested in. From the very beginning I had an understanding of what Chris found appealing about the novel.

Which was the magic and the . . .

Jonathan Nolan: It's funny because you said it in a way I hadn't quite found the words for. What I've been saying is it's a puzzle that collapses in on itself; but a trap is actually a fantastic word to describe what happens with these characters. You have these two very sharp guys who devote their considerable wit and talent to destroying each other.

This is sort of a cheesy question, but you are brothers and creative collaborators. Brothers are brothers, and they often compete. Was the competition aspect of this story an element that appealed to you two on a personal level?

Christopher Nolan: Not consciously. I sort of see that now, but I certainly was never conscious of it at all as I was working on the story. I think if you became self-conscious of [that aspect], it would mislead the writing process.

On the surface, this is a tale of rivalry between two master magicians. What is it about for you on a deeper, more allegorical level?

Jonathan Nolan: It's about obsession. I think on an allegorical level, when you're working on good material there's all sorts of rich thematic stuff that comes out of it. For me the appeal was the fun of it—the fun of the battle of wits, these two guys going after each other.

INTERVIEWER
When it comes to scripting, who's
better at what aspect of the craft?

JONATHAN NOLAN
I'm much better. I'm glad someone
finally asked that! I've been waiting
all morning.

INTERVIEWER
You know what I mean; is one guy
better at dialogue and the other at
plotting, for example?

JONATHAN NOLAN
What's galling to me is that, as much
as I'd like to think that because my
brother also directs these things,
somehow I would have an advantage
over him in screenwriting, but that's
not the case, despite the fact that
[writing] is my sole occupation.

What's cool about our relationship is
that growing up with different backgrounds and [in] different places,
our minds work in very similar
ways, but we're bringing different

experiences to bear. If you wanted
to oversimplify it, I'm the American
version and Chris is the English. I
can bounce ideas off of Chris and get
a sort of alternate-universe version
of what I might have written if I'd
grown up where he did.

It's an enormous luxury for me to
get material to a certain point and
then hand it off to Chris, or vice
versa, and it comes back richer and
deeper.

CHRISTOPHER NOLAN

This is different for different screenwriters, but I don't ever think of
screenwriting as separate components the way that studios sometimes like you to. I actually think of
screenwriting as being one thing, so
I don't think of it in terms of Jonathan being better at dialogue and me
at story or something like that. We
just throw the draft back and forth
as a whole thing.

So it's really just about making ideas better and perspectives richer?

Christopher Nolan: Yeah, I would say that's a good way of putting it. And also, because it's an honest collaboration—there are no hidden agendas or politics to it—the entire conversation is about what's best for the story.

Because we trust each other, it's a very open collaboration, and that's a very enjoyable thing and very good for the writing. Being a director [and] a writer, sometimes what you do is defend yourself against people who try to change what you've done. It's really essentially important to have a collaborator with whom you can be completely open to ideas and changes.

ADAM RAPP

CAREER HIGHLIGHTS:
Winter Passing; *In Treatment*

"I'm interested in having beginnings, middles, and ends to scenes for the actors and for myself, like a roadmap. But when it comes to the actual film, I use very little of the scene. The visual does so much—the eyes say so much more on film. I've just learned to trust that more with film writing."

—ADAM RAPP

As a screenwriter-director, novelist, and Pulitzer Prize–finalist playwright, Adam Rapp doesn't seem like a thug, but in his youth he was a total reprobate. While being raised by a single working mother in Joliet, Illinois, Rapp's favorite modes of self-expression included shoplifting and clipping hood ornaments from cars. The behavior won him a ticket to reform school and eventually a private military academy, where his tuition was only secured through athletic scholarships.

In what seems like a dream testimonial for military schools, by the age of twenty-four Rapp had not only earned an undergraduate degree, but had written *and published* his first novel, *Missing the Piano*.

Many awards, nearly thirty plays, a fistful of novels, a couple movies, and a television show later, something seems to have worked for him.

Here Rapp discusses his first film, *Winter Passing*, about an adrift, twenty-something actress (Zooey Deschanel) who returns to her childhood home to confront her mother's death, her fraught relationship with her writer-father (Ed Harris), his young student and admirer (Amelia Warner), and a strangely lost houseguest (Will Ferrell).

He talks about how screenwriting has made him a better writer in general, why he loves the character-driven screenplays of the seventies and why, when he's directing, he approaches his final film edit like rewriting a novel.

**What screenplays or films inspired you to write
Winter Passing?**

I love *Five Easy Pieces* and films of the seventies, particularly [films by] Hal Ashby and Bob Rafelson. I just
like that character-driven style that doesn't rely on pyro-
technics to entertain. Essentially, when I started *Winter
Passing*, I just wanted to make a '70s film.

**Since you work in the theater as well, do you feel that,
in a lot of ways, contemporary film talents like Charlie
Kaufman and Paul Thomas Anderson are making films
that are more like stage plays and that similarly, young
theater is more filmic—are the two merging?**

I totally agree. I was talking to a friend of mine, Jim
Ryan, who wrote and directed [the film] *The Young Girl
and the Monsoon* (1999), which started as a stage play.
He was saying that independent film has become the
new off-Broadway, which sort of deals in an indirect
way with your question.

It's true that you're seeing more character-driven stuff
that deals with people in a room talking to each other.
Even P. T. Anderson's stuff has a theatricality to it. His
characters have a kind of whimsy to them that used to
be really prevalent in off-Broadway theater. Now off-
Broadway has become stifled by investors that have to
farm an audience that's very conservative so they can
keep their theater financially afloat.

I do think it's also true that a lot of the new theater I'm seeing in New York feels more filmic. I have a friend who wrote a play, for example, that had sixty-four scenes, which is insane. When I read it, it read very much like a screenplay. On a broader level, I think we're being sort of conditioned culturally to let stories unfold at a much quicker light speed than they used to.

You've written in nearly every form. This being your first produced screenplay, what lessons did you take from the experience?

The thing I've discovered through my own process is that I'm writing full scenes with a beginning, middle, and end, but when I get into the editing room, I'm usually just using the middle. So I'm interested in having beginnings, middles, and ends to scenes for the actors and for myself, like a roadmap. But when it comes to the actual film, I use very little of the scene. The visual does so much, the camera focuses the eye of the viewer so much, that an expression on a face or just air between two people is so different than with two people in a theater. The eyes say so much more on film. I've just learned to trust that more with film writing.

INTERVIEWER
So it's like the old screenwriting cli-
ché: it's not what you write, it's what
you don't write?

ADAM RAPP
Absolutely. And trusting space without dialogue, whereas in the theater,
I need to use a lot of dialogue to
create the world the audience isn't
seeing.

Now, I [also] find I'm boiling my novels down more and more. I think the
film writing has really helped that.
I think for some weird reason, all
the forms I've written in have really
helped each other. I take craft from
each of them.

Having worked in theater and now having done this film, what's the most fun?

The most fun is working with the actors and shooting it. I love that. I mean, shooting almost kills you, so the athletic event of shooting, the decathlon of it, is exciting and makes for a kind of electricity on set. But having said that, I [also] really love the editing process because it's another manipulation. I can take all the footage I have and make my story even better. There's just so much you can do.

Film editing is a very writerly sort of process?

It's very writerly. I think it's like rewriting a novel, actually.

How do you feel about the final product of *Winter Passing*, and what lesson did you take from your first time through the process?

I loved shooting it and cutting it and working with the actors. I hated the politics of distribution; it was a nightmare. I wish that on no filmmaker.

It got ugly and I vowed to never make a film again for a while, but now that it's coming out, I am really pleased with the way it came out. I think after a few months that hunger to make another one returns.

SETH ROGEN AND EVAN GOLDBERG

CAREER HIGHLIGHTS:

Superbad; *Pineapple Express*; *Da Ali G Show*

"Judd Apatow really started to lay out for me his version of how you write a story, which is starting from an emotional thing that you've experienced, not even worrying if it's funny, and building the whole story on that."

—SETH ROGEN

Seth Rogen and his childhood pal Evan Goldberg started writing *Superbad* at age thirteen, shortly after meeting in bar mitzvah class (you *can* make this stuff up, but they didn't). Years later, under the mentorship of comedy kingpin Judd Apatow, they learned how to make the script not just funny, but good.

The two speak in that always-on, who's-gonna-say-the-funniest-joke-first way that veterans of comedy writers' rooms do. They exist in a weird, highly successful limbo between the stoned, guffawing class clowns they once were and the grown-up, A-list comedy writers (and in Rogen's case, actor) they've become. Among other things, they say Apatow taught them that to write a good comedy you have to start with an emotional truth you can build a story from, regardless of how funny it is.

And, whether or not it actually makes the script better, writing with someone is way more fun than doing it alone.

To what extent is *Superbad* a high school confessional or autobiography?

Seth Rogen: It's not autobiography, but it's definitely inspired by our lives. I was a loudmouthed dick in high school, and Evan was slightly less of a loud-mouthed dick. We both really wanted to get laid, which was not happening. So there are a lot of little things that are similar.

Evan Goldberg: Definitely. When friends and family see it, they almost all say, "That's a good Seth and that's a good Evan."

Can you each give me a one-line pitch to entice people to go see this film?

Evan Goldberg: Best fucking movie ever.

Seth Rogen: It's an oddly honest and sweet-but-filthy story about high school. I would go by the MPAA [Motion Picture Association of America] rating—that should motivate enough people.

You guys worked together on *Da Ali G Show*. How much of your writing routine on this film was based on that experience?

Evan Goldberg: One thing about that show that is unde-niable is that it was great for just hard-hitting jokes.

Seth Rogen: Yeah, we were just basically put in a room and asked to come up with two hundred hilarious questions to ask someone.

Evan Goldberg: It was like a comedy assembly line. The first seven days we were on fire and then we were like, "We have to keep doing this stuff?"

Seth Rogen: I remember thinking, "If I'm asked to write one more Bruno joke, I don't know what I'm going to do." I've literally written every gay Austrian joke I can possibly think of. But sometimes the funniest stuff comes after that point.

How about the actual structure needed for a feature, how have you come by that?

Evan Goldberg: When we first wrote *Superbad*, we didn't even have an outline.

Seth Rogen: We just wrote it.

Evan Goldberg: That's why it took twelve fucking years. That was another thing Judd Apatow helped us out with was structure. Specifically, he showed us a feature on the program Word where you could go into outline mode.

Huzzah!

Seth Rogen: When I started writing for *Undeclared* is when Judd really started to lay out for me his version of how you write a story, which is starting from an emotional thing that you've experienced, not even worrying if it's funny, and building the whole story on that. We almost had to rewrite the movie backwards. We liked all this stuff happening, but it was missing what would hopefully make it not just a funny movie but a *good* movie.

A coherent story?

Seth Rogen: Yeah. So we slowly came up with the fact that [the main characters] were going to different schools, focusing on the anxieties between them. We tried a lot of other things before that worked. But Judd showed me that for the first time on *Undeclared*. Evan moved down for a summer and we would just go to Judd's house and talk about writing all day long.

What funny writing inspires you guys, from film, TV, books, whatever?

Evan Goldberg: Growing up we were both influenced primarily by *Calvin and Hobbes*.

Seth Rogen: Yeah, that was probably the first funny thing I ever read when I was like eight.

Evan Goldberg: It was just the in-your-face sarcasm. I'd never experienced anything like that.

Seth Rogen: I went back and read it recently and it's like he's the most cynical kid in the entire universe. Rereading it again I realized, wow, this is where I drew my entire sense of humor. And then *The Simpsons* was as influential as anything could get humor-wise. It's been around almost our entire lives.

Evan Goldberg: When you're our age, it just kinda showed up and was perfect for how old we were and then it got smarter as we went along.

Are there any golden rules you've learned to the process of writing funny stuff?

Evan Goldberg: I've got one: bounce shit off everyone.

Seth Rogen: That's definitely a good idea.

Evan Goldberg: Just don't get cocky and think you got it right, because you probably didn't. Go to your friends and they'll tell you why.

Is that one of the reasons you two work together, because of the idea that you need a team to do comedy?

Evan Goldberg: Well, we have a relationship.

Seth Rogen: Yeah, it's 'cuz we love each other.

I mean aside from the sexual gratification.

Seth Rogen: It really just makes it fun. It makes it feel like it isn't work. My girlfriend's a writer and she doesn't have a writing partner and she's like, "Fuck, I wish I got to just sit around with my friend all day and write!" Writing's fun one way or another, but it's definitely better if you're not alone.

Obviously it's more fun, but on a practical level . . .

Seth Rogen: What's funny about us is that it's not like Evan's the story guy and I'm the comedy guy. We really don't have different skills than one another—we may not actually even write better together. It's just more enjoyable.

INTERVIEWER
But isn't comedy kind of unique; with
someone there you know instanta-
neously if something is funny or not.

SETH ROGEN
That's definitely true. We really are
just trying to make each other laugh.
If we both laugh our asses off, then
we put it in.

EVAN GOLDBERG
It's simple: Is anything really that
funny when you're alone? When I
watch *The Simpsons* with people,
I laugh my ass off the whole time.
When I watch it alone, I laugh out
loud maybe four times.

SETH ROGEN
Well then maybe it's actually bad
that we write together because we
think shit's funny that's not.

So at the end of the day, stuff's funnier with people.

Seth Rogen: Exactly. That's our message to the world: Things are funnier with people. Our message is simple and divine.

MELISSA ROSENBERG

CAREER HIGHLIGHTS:
The *Twilight* franchise; *Dexter*; *The O.C.*

"Thinking anything in writing is going to be easy is always a mistake. It is never easy. Writing is hard. If it wasn't hard, everyone would do it, right?"

—MELISSA ROSENBERG

In her tenure as sole scripter on the *Twilight* franchise, Melissa Rosenberg experienced the screenwriting equivalent of the heady, harrowing arc of Bella Swan, the adorably mortal heroine at the heart of the spectacularly popular teen vampire bestsellers-turned-blockbusters.

Here she talks in the midst of adapting the fourth and final book, the 900-page bone-rattler *Breaking Dawn*, into two separate films simultaneously, and just before the release of *The Twilight Saga: Eclipse*.

Rosenberg has maintained her breakneck pace on the vampire franchise since late 2007, when she was tapped to adapt Stephenie Meyer's maiden book in the series. Not only did she turn that script around in a little more than two months, but she's done the bulk of the franchise while juggling her role as coexecutive producer of the hit Showtime series *Dexter*. Lack of time and the enormity of writing two scripts at once for *Breaking Dawn* finally drove her to leave *Dexter*, a show she counts as the best of her television career.

During this nearly immortal effort, she's relied on an outline-first approach. With adaptations especially, she says you must find your "big moments" and then build everything on that chronological framework. She has also proved a classic writing truism: if you're given more time to write, you'll wind up using it, whether or not it actually makes the finished script better.

You're in the midst of your two-part adaptation of *Break-ing Dawn*, the final films of the *Twilight* series. You've said that, at least initially, you thought *Eclipse* would be easier?

That was actually from the outset, separate from *Break-ing Dawn*. Looking at the first three books, it seemed like it would be easier just because it had all this action. Of course, that was wrong. Thinking anything in writing is going to be easy is always . . .

A mistake?

Always a mistake. It is never easy. Writing is hard. If it wasn't, everyone would do it, right?

True. *Eclipse* has a lot of action but it's mainly in the third act.

Exactly.

That didn't really help you in terms of the first two acts. Tell me what you had to do with those first two acts to lead up to that big conflict.

It was about taking that threat and building on it to the third-act conflict. The entire book is from Bella's point of view, so anything that happens in the book, she hears about after the fact, [when] she's not actually present. With the script, I don't have that restriction. I could actu-ally go away from her point of view occasionally, so I was able to build a few of those scenes that she hears about after the fact and invent a few to help build to this conflict, which, hopefully, helps to keep that sense of threat impending and growing throughout [the first two acts].

This *Twilight* phenomenon has happened really fast, but it's also been, what, three and half years now that you've been ensconced in this?

Yeah. It was about two months before the Writers strike.

That's right. That's an interesting benchmark for this.

Yeah.

During all that time has your process for breaking down these books remained the same?

I've used the same system that I've had from the beginning. The only thing that's changed is that I've involved Stephenie Meyer a little more in my process. I've used her as a resource more and more as I've gone along.

So that has increased as you've gone along?

Yes it has and our relationship has developed over the time, but my process has remained the same all the way through.

You're adapting these books, but getting as invested as you have, as attached to these characters and these scripts, you must start to feel some sense of ownership as an author too.

> I've certainly become very invested but I give all props to Stephenie. I would not have the career I now have without her, so I take nothing from that, certainly.

Of course. And going back for a minute, can you encapsulate what your process has been for breaking these books?

> The first thing I do is I read the book through, and I sit back and sort of let come to mind what pops. What I'm looking for there is structure; you know, what emerges as the mid-point, what are the arcs of the characters and how best to structure them. I let the scenes wash over me to decide what the big moments are.

> Then I start building from there. The way I do that is to put into a very abbreviated few pages what the key scenes in the book are, chapter by chapter. Once I have my structure of what the basic acts are, I start filling in the muscle and sinew.

And did *Eclipse* take comparatively less or more time than the others?

> Well, to some extent, it's [been a matter of] how much time I have. I did have a little bit more time with *Eclipse*. With *Twilight*, we were fighting the strike dead-

line, so I slammed that one out. With *New Moon* I had
more time but I was juggling *Dexter* at the same time.

How fast did you do *Twilight*?

I think I outlined for about a month, while simultaneously working on *Dexter,* and then it was five weeks to
write the script.

Geez!

Yeah.

And then with *New Moon* you had . . . ?

New Moon was over the course of about six months, but
you've gotta understand, that's two days a week.

Right, because you're doing *Dexter* . . .

So it's two days a week times six months.

No one's sayin' you're a slacker here, believe me.

And then *Eclipse* was done when *Dexter* was on hiatus . . .
I did rewrites when it came back.

**So for this one you were luxuriating in time, relatively
speaking?**

Yeah, although I had to take a few months off to just regenerate a little.

Did it actually make it harder having the luxury of a little time and being able to focus on just the one script?

Well, I was still under the gun with *Eclipse* because I knew *Dexter* was coming back and I had to get it done. But with *Breaking Dawn* now I have that for the first time. I have left *Dexter*. I had to, knowing that *Breaking Dawn* was probably going to be two movies. I can do one *Twilight* and *Dexter*, but I couldn't do two.

So I very sadly left *Dexter*, because that show was my favorite television experience to date, and I've had many.

But it's true that when I don't have time pressures I don't use my time as wisely. It's a so much nicer way to write and it allows me time for creative contemplation, which is great, but sometimes I find myself just kind of surfing the Web and I'm like, "Wow, three hours just passed."

I'm not sure. On the one hand, perhaps I'm coming up with more ideas because I have time. Maybe the work is better. Then again, maybe it's not because I'm not as disciplined.

And looking ahead to *Breaking Dawn*, where are you with it now?

Deep in the center [*laughs*].

INTERVIEWER

Now that you're in the midst of this final couplet of films and the end is in sight, what are your feelings contemplating this being done?

MELISSA ROSENBERG

Well, it's interesting. For the past four years I've been writing *Dexter* and one *Twilight* or another. Both projects have been amazing experiences, the best of my career. I know both of these worlds really well, [and] I know the characters' voices, [and] I'm comfortable living in their worlds. That has been hard won. I've spent many, many years trying to find a home and then I found two.

So that's hard to leave. It's a nice feeling; confidence is a nice feeling. And yet I'm excited to see what's next—nervous about it, but very excited to see what I can do next.

GARY
ROSS

CAREER HIGHLIGHTS:
The Hunger Games; *Big*; *Seabiscuit*

"You're never done writing. You're never done discovering the movie. You have to be patient enough to let the movie talk to you and to listen to it, to not try to freeze dry whatever your first version was or try to defend it. It's a living thing and it's going to keep changing and talking to you and you have to listen."

—GARY ROSS

Other than the fact that they're nearly all hugely successful, the motley menagerie of scripts Academy Award–nominated writer/director Gary Ross has written are unified by one thing: they're character-driven stories moored deeply to an emotive core.

Whether it's his whimsically winning debut *Big* (which he co-wrote with Anne Spielberg), or the Oscar-nodded horse-racing biopic *Seabiscuit*, or the animated story of a misfit mouse in *The Tale of Despereaux*, Ross looks for an emotional center to fuel his story.

He found that center again when his twin son and daughter turned him on to Suzanne Collins's hit young-adult book series *The Hunger Games*. For all its futurism and supercharged action, he saw the story of a teenage girl learning to trust. His instinctive sense of the story's heart showed in his first draft of a script, which won him a fan in Collins.

Here, during a conversation about writing and directing *The Hunger Games*, Ross expounds on the joy of collaborating, his total belief in the creative power of outlining, and why any writer who says a character is telling him where the script should go might be in trouble.

With regard to *The Hunger Games*, Suzanne Collins has said that your draft really nailed the emotional arc, particularly between Katniss and Peeta, in a way that had not been captured in other drafts. How did you zero in on this emotional center?

I wrote a draft of my own which was very faithful to the book. Subsequent to that Suzanne read it, liked it a lot, gave me some notes and came out to visit me in California. We started talking to one another even though we weren't working together on it yet and that conversation was so electric and spontaneous that within about an hour we were working together.

As far as the question of zeroing in on the emotional center, to me the story was the arc of someone who trusts no one and who ultimately learns to trust. [Katniss is someone] who has made herself as invulnerable as possible, kind of steeled herself off from the world. But she's someone who learns to trust, develops a sense of empathy, and learns to care.

The great irony of the story is that [learning to trust] makes her stronger rather than weaker . . . that was a very interesting idea to me. I saw the whole mistrust of Peeta as a really interesting aspect of the book. Here was somebody who has such a guileless, open, unending love for her that she mistrusts it. This is also something that's resonant outside the Hunger Games that's very interesting.

So that's just kind of what I wrote to. That was my compass setting.

Obviously an emotional arc is always crucial to drama, but do you think it's even more crucial with material like this that can become so special effects–focused?

The emotional center of a movie is always the most important thing. I don't think it's particular to this story. I do think it makes a story like this so much more resonant, richer, and a much fuller experience when it has something strong on it's mind and has such a strong emotional core.

One of the things that drew me to make this movie, both as a writer and a director, was that it was a phenomenal character piece at the same time. Yes it has this massive canvas of this hideous spectacle being put on by the Capitol, but there's also such a personal story and it's an acting piece.

When you're able to make a movie on this big a canvas but have that strong and emotional core, you're lucky.

And as the director, you're in an interesting position here where you can lean the story ultimately in many directions . . .

I've always tried to find the emotional underpinning of whatever I've done—*Big, Dave, Seabiscuit,*

Pleasantville, whatever they are. In this situation, it's one of the things that drew me to it. The area of the movie that I was interested in doing and that moved me the most was the death of Rue, when [Katniss] memorializes this little girl and honors her life and her death. That was a scene I couldn't wait to write and to direct, that relationship between those two girls.

Do you feel there are any themes here that are apropos of our time?

There are a lot of things. This book has a lot on its mind. The whole idea that entertainment can be used as a means of political control, I think is fascinating. That entertainment has evolved into this hideous spectacle is really interesting . . . We've created our version of the Arena, writ small. Suzanne was able to extrapolate on those things and realize how resonant they were.

I also think there's something deeper going on here, [which is] how much can you trust? How vulnerable can you be? Does opening yourself up make you weaker or stronger? I think that has appeal in general and particularly to teenagers.

That's Katniss's journey. It ultimately leads to self-sacrifice and discovery of her own humanity and her own ethics. She reaches an ethical line that she just will not cross and that makes the piece resonant.

Before *The Hunger Games* you hadn't really had a writing partner since Anne Spielberg on *Big*, is that right?

Annie and I had a wonderful time together on *Big*. This was a much briefer experience because I wrote the first draft by myself and then Suzanne came in and polished that with me. But just being in a room with someone again and having a great writer to bounce stuff off of, to share that give and take, was really a lot of fun. Experiencing other people's methodologies is wonderful.

So it was refreshing after all these years since *Big*.

Yeah, I mean, I've written a lot of solitary screenplays since *Big—Dave, Seabiscuit, Pleasantville, Despereaux . . .* that was a lot of time to spend alone in a room. To be with someone was wonderful. And, of course with Suzanne, this is her creation, this is her world. She has so much at her fingertips, she's a compendium of all this knowledge.

Suzanne is also wonderful about not only being able to translate into another medium and not being precious about what's on the written page, but about finding excitement in the adaptation process. We had a great time together.

INTERVIEWER

I know you're a big outliner. To
outline or not to outline is an oft-
debated subject among screenwriters.
You consider the outlining process
the place where the discovery happens. But I'm curious if you've ever
found yourself discovering stuff later
and—

GARY ROSS

Yeah, I discover stuff at every phase
of the process. I now consider the
shooting and editing of the movie
a further extension of the writing.
You're never done writing. You're
never done discovering the movie.
You have to be patient enough to let
the movie talk to you and to listen
to it, to not try to freeze dry whatever your first version was or try to
defend it. It's a living thing and it's
going to keep changing and talking to
you and you have to listen.

Having said that, I believe the
first step has to be an outline. You
wouldn't build a house without blue-
prints. It doesn't mean that it's a less
creative part of the process. It can be

a more creative part of the process
and, to my mind, the most creative
part of the process is where the bigger decisions are made. By the end of
the movie, you're down to the color
timing. You're affecting it minutely.

At the beginning of a movie there
are so many large conceptual ideas
in play about how to approach the
material. That can be a very exciting time if you don't get tense and
think, "Oooh, what's my outline?
What's my story?" like it's some
kind of dry clinical document. If
you let it have life and you're open
to the same sort of discovery that
many people assume happens in the
screenplay, that can be a wonderful
and exciting time.

So, for you, outlining is a creatively explosive, rich time?

Tremendously creative. First of all, you're not bound to a linear structure . . . you're not gonna hit page thirteen after twelve, page fourteen after page thirteen. You're not bound to be on the part of the train track you're on.

Secondly, it hasn't been formed yet. The decisions are all up in the air. The horizons are broader and there's more you can do with it than when you're locked into the writing process, per se. By definition it's more creative if you can be open to the possibilities.

You've also said that, in essence, characters are servants to the story.

Well, that's been a bit misquoted . . .

Okay, that's good to know, but it's not about the quote so much. What do you think about screenwriters that say they let the characters show them where they want to go?

I find that charming, the fact that they feel these fictional creations of theirs are living, breathing entities. I don't mean that in a sarcastic way at all. I think it's delightful that they're hearing them. But what they're hearing is themselves expressed through a character, by definition, because they're the ones creating the character. It's a way of listening to yourself and your own intentions.

The only point I was ever making about character being subordinate to the whole is that you never want the script to become just a mouthpiece for the rhetoric of a single character. A script is a dialectic coming from a conflict between characters and their situations —the way they collide and hate each other and love each other. It's the characters in collision with one another that produces a third thing, and that third thing is the work.

Often when people say, "I let my characters tell me what to do," I get very nervous because frequently that means one of those characters is a mouthpiece for the author's point of view, instead of having the author's point of view played out dramatically through conflict in front of us.

Big was your first produced script and was kind of like hitting a grand slam your first time up. How much did that affect you as a screenwriter?

I had labored for a while. I think I was twenty-seven when I wrote _Big_, but I'd been trying to write since I was twenty or twenty-one years old. Even though it all seems very young to me now that I'm in my fifties, at the time I felt like I'd languished in the woods without any recognition for a while. So when it came it was pretty welcome.

I really loved the story. I was very gratified in the way
that you are whenever you put something into the world
that people connect to. There's great satisfaction in that.
Because it was the first time, it felt very special to me.
But it didn't really mess my head up.

**Did you always know how you were going to proceed
from the early success of *Big*? Did you have a plan to not
repeat it?**

Listen, there are many people who would accuse me
of doing that with *Dave*. I remember when I won the
Scripter award for *Seabiscuit*, Callie Khouri (Oscar winner for *Thelma and Louise*) and Paul Attanasio (Academy Award–nominated for *Donnie Brasco* and *Quiz
Show*) presented me the award and they took the opportunity to roast me. Callie said, "It's so great that Gary
found Laura Hillenbrand (author of *Seabiscuit*); otherwise he'd be doing another one of those conked-on-the-
head movies where people wake up as someone else."

I thought that was pretty funny.

**Do you feel like the continuing box office dominance of
special-effects-driven "event" movies makes it harder to
maintain the emotional arc in a script?**

No, I don't think so. If you look at last year how many
interesting character-based dramas there were: *Black
Swan* or *True Grit* or *The Fighter*. Everybody kept get-

ting surprised. Or look at the success of *The Help*. These are character-based stories and they're not comedies, they're dramas. And they all made of ton of money and were incredibly popular. So I don't think it's so.

I think we like to say that because it's an anxiety, but I don't think character-driven stories are on the wane. We may act surprised every time they're successful, but they're not on the wane.

TERRY ROSSIO
AND
TED ELLIOTT

CAREER HIGHLIGHTS:
The Pirates of the Caribbean franchise; *Shrek*; *The Mask of Zorro*

Terry Rossio: "We don't make big blockbuster movies. We make small, intimate character studies that happen to . . ."

Ted Elliott: "Cost 150 million dollars!"

In today's Hollywood, big studios are almost entirely focused on the "event" film—the blockbuster, the tent-pole, the franchise. Though it rarely gets the respect it deserves, writing these films not only takes elephant skin but serious chops.

Call it the art of the franchise.

Terry Rossio and Ted Elliott are masters of that art. Talking about *Dead Man's Chest*, the second installment of the $4 billion *Pirates of the Caribbean* franchise, they ardently proclaim they aren't writing blockbusters, just great stories with great characters. They say they constantly strive to break formula. They also think multiple writers aren't necessarily a bad thing, as long as the writers get to choose who they work with at the start of a project.

As for those elitist critics who sometimes call their plots formulaic, if such a formula exists, they'd love to get it because it would save them a ton of work.

When writing the sophomore installment of a franchise like *Pirates*, after the first has been such a smash, some would say you can't lose. Others would say it's much harder. What's the truth?

Ted Elliott: Gore Verbinski (director of the first three *Pirates* films) put it best when he said that we were nuts to be doing this because the only thing that anybody will recognize is if we fail [*laughs*].

Terry Rossio: Yes, the expectations are high. Yes, people are saying it's going to be the number one film of the summer and it's going to be great. But there are no guarantees. You can just look at the fan reaction to *Matrix 2* or *Indiana Jones and the Temple of Doom*. It's like the saying, "Certainty cometh before the fall."

Those high expectations made it all the more difficult to do the second, because you don't have the element of people having a delightful first meeting with characters in a world for the first time.

You don't have the fun of the first blush?

Terry Rossio: Exactly. The higher the expectations created by the first movie, the harder it is to meet them with fewer tools at your disposal.

But by the same token, you now have known, popular characters with back stories to play with. Did you discover any advantages within this framework?

Ted Elliott: Yes, because of the unanticipated level of response audiences had to the first one, they have created in their minds what they expect the second one to be. We can actually take advantage of that to surprise them.

Terry Rossio: Another advantage of the strong audience response to the first one is, obviously, that you have more money to make the second one. You can build an extra ship [*laughs*], that sort of thing. It's not a bad thing to have a built-in audience and to feel that you're gonna get your first weekend. Our concern as screenwriters is to deliver the second and third weekend.

INTERVIEWER
What is it about screenwriting, particularly for big popcorn movies and comedies, that lends itself to the team approach?

TERRY ROSSIO
We don't make big blockbuster movies. We make small, intimate character studies that happen to . . .

TED ELLIOTT
Cost a 150 million dollars! [laughs]

TERRY ROSSIO
Well, that become really popular. Every movie that we've worked on, at some point, felt like a disaster. It felt like it was either weird or odd or too risky. It's only after that, that people start saying, "When you were working on this blockbuster movie . . ."

We remember working on stories that were blocky and difficult and that could've failed completely.

TED ELLIOTT

Terry's least favorite criticism, which
shows up all the time, is that we
wrote a "by-the-numbers plot." Could
I get a book of those numbers? It
sure would have made it easier when
we were sitting in that office, struggling for a way to get from point A
to point C. We'd have said, "Oh, B! Of
course!"

TERRY ROSSIO

These films are a lot more complex
than they seem.

I don't mean that question disparagingly. It's just that when you're working on a film that's in that vein . . .

Ted Elliot: The movies that Terry and I like to write happen to be those kind of movies. The question I think you're leading to is, "Have you thought about doing any personal, darker stories?" The answer is no. The writers who do those do them really well, and we do this really well. This is what we like to write.

Terry Rossio: There are good storytelling techniques that you might use for *One Flew Over the Cuckoo's Nest* or *Network*—films that are considered in the category of what might be called Academy Award bait.

If you happen to then [be writing] a swashbuckler or a genre film or a science fiction film or whatever, you don't say, "This is a popcorn movie, so I'm going to use different techniques." What we try to do is find an interesting story and use whatever those techniques are. Then, as it turns out, if you do a genre movie and use all the normal writing techniques, like, *make it good,* all of the sudden it becomes this blockbuster popcorn thing. The intent is to treat every story as something that requires the same narrative ambition that any story would require.

Do you see any clear trends with the storytelling for these event movies?

Ted Elliott: What you're looking at with a big-budget movie is a huge capital expenditure. In order to justify that risk, the studio has to calculate for the best possible return. That's where you run into trouble with good stories. A lot of times a good story is a story that hasn't been told before in that way.

Our approach with *Pirates,* for example, was to say, "Look, there are things audiences will respond to. All we gotta do is find a good story that needs those things to happen." One of the reasons I was happy with the success of the first one and how this one has turned out, is that other writers can point to it and say, "See, it worked there."

You don't have to worry about the audience following every single story point, you don't have to worry about, "Hey, that guy just kicked a dog through a hedge; it's gonna make him unlikable." You just have to make it interesting and involving.

And I know what you're talking about with independent film; it's stopped being an economic statement, it's become an aesthetic. But it's the same thing [with independent films]: Be interesting. That's more important than being liked. Break formulas. Be aware what the expectations are, but use them to your advantage.

Terry Rossio: I have a bit of a radical answer to your question and it's more about process: There's a trend, I want to call it the Pixar model. You look at Pixar films and they'll have four writers on a movie. They have a process up there of having multiple talents on a movie, almost like a think tank.

I think in the past there were these brilliant directors who held the whole movie in their head and brilliant writers who could conceive of a whole world full-blown. Maybe there aren't as many of those talents around, and in order to satisfy that need for blockbusters, we will be gravitating toward more of a team approach, when needed.

There's obviously a difference between a bunch of people doing multiple rewrites versus working as a team from the start.

Terry Rossio: There's a difference, but the effect is the same. It is actually legit to have a singular-vision movie that multiple writers worked on.

Ted Elliott: If writers end up in a situation of serial collaboration, there are two ways to do it: one at a time, without any interaction, which is the feature model, or to presume serial collaboration where needed from the start, which is the staff model of television.

Terry Rossio: And animation.

Ted Elliot: Terry and I are looking to see if there is a way for writers to take more control of the development itself by saying at the outset, "Okay, here are the other writers we're going to work with." It's a different model. It would basically be, writers own the writers' building [*laughs*], if you see what I mean.

ERIC
ROTH

CAREER HIGHLIGHTS:

Forrest Gump; Ali; The Horse Whisperer; The Insider

"It will come to you, whether it's in a dream or some song you hear or a feeling you have or some memory. I don't know what the reasons are, whether they're subconscious or unconscious, but something always seems to save the day."

—ERIC ROTH

Eric Roth speaks in an almost tepid tone, like a weary man thinking out loud in an empty room. But it's not apathy. The Oscar-winning scripter's pleasantly rumpled, modest manner stems from a thoughtful mind that long ago realized a distaste for loud speakers with little to say.

So, like a Zen master who never wanted to be asked, the veteran writer answers questions in a bare, hovering voice that makes you listen more carefully for all its quietness. Of course, what he says helps hold listeners after they lean in. There is also the matter of his career, as notable for huge successes as for the genre-jumping diversity of his credits, from *Forrest Gump* to *The Horse Whisperer* and *The Insider* to *Ali*.

A good story is what connects them all.

Here, in an expansive, at times personal chat, Roth talks about *The Curious Case of Benjamin Button*, his own mortality, and the unavoidable truth of classic dramatic structure.

He says he writes more to theme than he does to story and that the first twenty or so pages of a script are where all the work happens. He rewrites those first pages over and over until he breaks the script and knows where it goes from there.

Was the scope and time frame of this narrative [of *The Curious Case of Benjamin Button*] as similar to *Forrest Gump* as it seems like it might have been?

> I guess you could say that, but you could also probably say *Ali* is like that. I think it's not inaccurate, but this is really from cradle to grave and *Forrest Gump* isn't. It was certainly from a boy to a man.

To what extent was the scope reminiscent of work you'd done before, or was it a pretty singular experience?

> I tried to make it singular, let's put it that way. Whatever is reminiscent is not by design.

Right, and I don't mean to say that . . .

> No, no, I think it's a fair question because obviously I created both, so I'm bringing something with me. There's probably some similarity in style, but I think they're very different movies. I think *Benjamin* deals with different subjects.

What is this story about to you?

> I think it's a look at mortality in a way, the natural qualities of life and death. There's nothing really extraordinary about his life except for the fact that it's extraordinary because he ages backwards. He's sort of an ordinary man in extraordinary circumstances.

Other than being a novelty, what does the fact that he ages backwards do to the story?

I think it makes you think about all sorts of things. On face value, you'd think it would be great. You'd become young again, you'd have great vision again and great stamina and great love, things that sound sort of wondrous. And yet, when one would experience it, it seems to me there is a major component of loneliness. And also, you're simply aging toward your demise in a different way.

The simple conclusion, without giving too much of the movie away, is that, whether you live your life backwards or forwards, it's best to live it well.

How did this story strike you on a personal level?

I can talk to you about my parents' death. They both died during the writing of this. They informed the whole writing of this.

Oh, I didn't know that.

That's why I was a little hesitant [when you asked earlier on background] about them . . . I don't want to . . . I love them.

Did they pass in the same year?

They passed about three years apart, but the [writing] process began when my mother was passing away. I'm not trying to be exploitive of either of their deaths, but it did make me a more mature writer. It's like the Joan Didion quote about how you have to go to this land of grief that you're not prepared to go to, but that you have to go to when a loved one dies.

When your parents die it's obviously a very unique brand of grief because you're losing a person that's beloved, but it also must bring up questions of your own mortality.

Completely. I remember one particular day, my son, who was twenty-five or so at the time, was having a child and my father had had a stroke so they were at the same hospital. I was going from one room to another. So my son having a child makes me a grandfather and I'm also a son going to visit his father. It just happened that they all fell at the same time.

That does bring up your mortality. Look, I know I'm not only on deck, I'm up to bat right now. But that's not necessarily bad. If one believes in the natural qualities of life and death, there's nothing wrong with it. That's one of the things about the movie that we deal with.

That story you describe in the hospital sounds so Buttonesque, literally going from your newborn grandchild to your father. And this was right at the beginning of the writing process?

This was more in the middle of it.

Did you feel the universe was messing with you at all?

I don't know . . . I'm not sure the universe is that interested in me. I think you just hopefully come to terms with the conditions of life. There's going to be all sorts of experiences—good, bad, and indifferent. You have to face these things.

Is it a matter of acceptance?

Yeah. I mean, I'm not telling you I'm all that accepting, but I think acceptance is key to some form of peace. But what would I know?

Well, you might know a few things.

I don't think I know anything. I really don't. Not any more than anyone else.

Because of your parents' passing, your new grandchild, and writing this movie, did the completion of this script feel different than other films you've written?

Yeah, I would say more than anything else I've written, this one is the most personal. It's also one that has helped me find some acceptance. That's a great question. I love that.

If you can get technical for a minute, with this particular story, what was your first step in terms of grappling with it given its scope and its source material?

There were two, I think. One was trying to decipher what I was going to use from the short story, which became almost nothing. That was painful because obviously F. Scott Fitzgerald is a hundred times the writer I could ever be. But I had to make a decision about what spoke to me in doing this.

I knew that he had written this as a whimsy. I spoke to a few of his biographers and neither felt that he thought this was one of his important works. It was something that had been dashed off.

INTERVIEWER

Was it important for you to know
that?

ERIC ROTH

Well, to me it was. Most important
was the core of it, which is the idea
of a man aging backwards, which
actually came from an essay Mark
Twain had written about how interesting it would be if we could age the
other way and avoid all the infirmi-
ties of old age. Maxwell Perkins, F.
Scott's editor, gave him the [Twain]
essay, and he wrote a story for a
magazine. He'd also just had a baby
so he probably needed some money
for diapers and alcohol.

Diapers and booze: a classic combo.

Diapers and booze, what else is there? So eighty years
later it's given to me. A number of people had taken a
shot at it, including the wonderful Robin Swicord, but
for whatever reason it hadn't really landed. So they gave
me a little bit of free rein.

**So despite F. Scott Fitzgerald's story and Robin Swicord's
previous drafts, you were essentially operating with a
blank slate except for the general concept?**

Yes.

**Having dealt with the decision about the source material,
what was the next step?**

The next thing was finding the theme, which is something I'm always interested in. As I said earlier, I wanted
to tell a story that lent itself to the idea that, whether you
live your life backwards or forwards, you should live it
well. That's how I wanted to tell the story.

The next step was the technical decision of how I
wanted to tell the story, which was through a framing
device. It doesn't feel like a device, I think it feels very
natural being told by this old woman who's dying.
Once I had that, I knew what the beginning and end was
because I knew what was going to happen to her. I knew
I was going to start it with a baby being born under

unusual circumstances. I decided I was going to take the story through his life—with jumps in time and all—but that it would go from cradle to grave, or grave to cradle as it were.

So first off you found your sort of thematic ethos?

Which, if you want to talk about screenwriting, is true of all my work. I'm as interested in the theme as I am in what the story is. I feel like I write more toward theme than I do toward story.

Once you comprehend your theme, it sort of navigates you through the narrative?

Yeah, I think it does. Then I start to populate it. Part of the storytelling is all these people that come through your life. Some make an impact and some don't. And in the long run, these people have helped give you your point of view on life. It's this pastiche of people that helps create the fabric of who you are.

Also, you might find it interesting with this movie, I don't think there's a bad person in it. There are complicated people and people who don't live up to what we'd hoped they'd be, but nobody really arch, I hope.

How much did this population of characters refer to people you've known?

I don't think too much except for the woman dying. There are all kinds of personal things that enter into it, but no specific people, I think, except for her. And then there are several metaphorical things about destiny and chance and fate, which is an overriding thing.

And the woman telling the story is referential to your mother?

Completely. Some of it, I just used actual words she said to me. When she was dying I asked her if she was afraid and she said, "No, I'm curious." That's in the movie.

And then there's the notion, what if a person is telling you things you didn't know about them in the last moments of their life? There was nothing startling about my mother at the end of her life that she hadn't told me, but you still sort of learn things about people as they're going away that makes you appreciate them even more.

So you go from theme to characters . . .

Then I had to think about the story. The storytelling is very picaresque. It has a structure, but it's very episodic. I've done that in a couple films before, even though I can write in the classical, three-act dramatic structure.

Structure is so dominant in modern screenwriting. It's obviously crucial to effective screenwriting, but how do you balance it against emotion, abstraction, and originality in a script?

I don't think you can avoid the classical dramatic structure. You can stand on your head and try to have four acts instead of three, but you're still going to have a beginning that presents a problem, a second act that complicates it, and a third or fourth [act] that resolves it or doesn't resolve it. I don't think you can escape it.

Sure, in that macro sense, but on a more micro sense, during the actual writing process some approaches are more reliant on mapping and outlining the skeletal structure to feed the narrative, versus the narrative feeding the structure.

Yeah, with me, even though I'm well aware of structure and where the act breaks should be, the narrative is first. It's difficult to say which is the chicken and which is the egg. You know, in the back of your head that the structure is there, the act, and so forth.

Do you think you've gotten better over the years at translating your creative intention to the form?

I don't know if I've gotten better. In some cases I've probably gotten longer and I think I'm more confident. I've always been somewhat self-assured, but as I've gotten older I've developed more of a confidence.

If I have any sort of strength it's that I'm willing to fail.
I've always been willing to try things that may not work,
which probably comes from a hint of arrogance.

**Is there any single thing you've honed in your process over
the years that seems most significant to you? Something
that if you could go back, you wish you had understood?**

I think probably patience. I was more impatient before
about trying to make things occur creatively. Now I'm
less frustrated by that. I just think it will come.

You're not muscling the creative process?

I'm not forcing square pegs into round holes. It will
come to you, whether it's in a dream or some song you
hear or a feeling you have or some memory. I don't
know what the reasons are, whether they're subconscious or unconscious, but something always seems to
save the day.

You just have to be there and wait?

Yeah, I think waiting is really important. I mean, it's not
like I'm waiting. I keep doing it every day. I go back to
page one and start writing again. All scripts I start, I just
keep writing the first twenty pages, the first chapter until
I get it right and then I know what the rest of the script
should be.

It's amazing how every screenwriter seems to have that tipping point where the script is cracked. For some it's the outline, for some the first full draft.

> It is amazing. I don't ever wonder, "How am I going to get from page twenty-five to page eighty-five?" All of the sudden you're just there [at page twenty-five] and then it's sort of a dream in a way. You feel completely satisfied with what you're going to end up doing; you feel, "This is great. Now I can end this, and all these things I've started can take off in a way."

Sounds as if the hard part is getting to that point in the process where the wind comes around behind you.

> I guess everyone gets there differently. Because it takes me so long to finish my first draft, it's probably similar to some other screenwriter's fifth draft because it takes me so long to get through round one.

You do your drafting in those first twenty pages or so?

> Yeah, exactly.

JAMES SCHAMUS

CAREER HIGHLIGHTS:
Co-president of Focus Features; *The Ice Storm*; *Lust, Caution*

"If you really wanna bore everyone around you and never have sex again in your life, just go to a party and say, 'What is indie film?' But 99.999 percent of the genetic code that makes a successful independent movie, I hate to tell ya, is the same as what makes a successful studio movie: It's called narrative."

—JAMES SCHAMUS

If you've always dreamed of living a life in the film biz and are wondering why you aren't, it may be because James Schamus is living it for you. He's only one bow-tied, bespectacled man of modest stature, but this screenwriter and co-founder of Focus Features has managed to excel at nearly a half-dozen, at times contradictory, careers in film simultaneously.

He is essentially an art house geek, able to spin the berets off the most studied avant-garde film aficionados; he's also a Berkeley PhD and Columbia professor (the bow tie and spectacles really help here). But he's a screenwriter too, and, somewhat astonishingly, at the same time he's also the shrewd, fast-talking, executive head of a studio-owned film company.

Aren't writers and studio execs mortal enemies?

To many, yes. But to Schamus this seemingly soul-splitting oxymoron is just a bunch of hyperbole. In all his incarnations, Schamus says he's simply striving to do the same thing: bring rare perspectives and fine cinematic art to more people. It's a mission accomplished with offerings like *Lost in Translation, The Ice Storm, Milk,* and *Brokeback Mountain*—"little" movies that have left a huge mark on cinema culture.

During a sprawling, at times beret-spinning conversation based around his script for the Ang Lee–helmed film *Taking Woodstock,* Schamus talks Aristotle, the endless debate over the soul of independent film, and how good stories with strong voices are all that really matters.

There are many facets to Elliot Tiber's memoir [*Taking Woodstock*] that we'll get to, but let's focus on this young man who, in an attempt to save his parents' motel, essentially gave Woodstock a place to happen. For you as a screenwriter, what were the big themes or narrative engines of this story?

The great challenge of *Taking Woodstock* is the kind of un-American protagonist. The character of Elliot Tiber fulfills what Aristotle would have called a sufficient cause, not a necessary cause. That distinction between sufficient and necessary cause has provided a great deal of energy to American movies—we love our heroes to be the necessary cause of things, not the sufficient one. And yet the pleasures of centering a film around a [sufficient hero] are many.

What turns you on creatively about the sufficient hero?

What's exciting about that for this particular material— not always—is that you're talking about a moment in time when people took seriously the idea that you could be happy by letting things happen. Letting it happen, rather than making it happen, was just as positive an idea.

There is a kind of happiness—and the word "happiness" is etymologically linked to the word "happen"— in accepting things. So it's a movie about accepting things. Acceptance is sometimes a little different from doing, right?

Is it important, then, for the whole paradigm of "letting things happen," that the protagonist be sufficient rather than necessary?

Exactly. It's part of the overall joy of the thing. It also allows you a certain kind of comedic tone.

Do you think letting things happen is making a comeback?

Wow. I'll leave that to you and the audiences.

Don't do that. But with current worldwide hardships and the sense of reevaluation, do you think this idea is a little more relevant to audiences right now?

Sure. But you know, the great news about making movies with Ang is, we don't need to please a lot of people, make our profit, and move on to the next one.

I do think that, in terms of the critical establishment, this is going to be a little bit of a head spin, seeing Ang not taking things too seriously and having some fun, kind of letting the movie happen. I think that will take some people by surprise.

You are a singular master in the industry of taking an off-formula story and bringing it to a focused (pardon the pun) place where it can reach a much wider audience. How conscious are you as a writer and an exec of tuning the material to where you can get a bigger audience, not that we're talking about popcorn blockbusters here . . . there seems to be some kind of algebra to it?

Here's how it works. There's no algebra to it or formula but there is an attitude. I was trying to formulate that myself. I would say the following: We're always taking stuff from outside of the mainstream and, without pandering to the mainstream, we're just facing toward them for the conversation.

A lot of my favorite movies are very avant-garde works of film art. The conversation that they propose is a conversation to be had only with the people inside that world, which is fine. I'm partially in that world and I appreciate it. What we try to do is, instead of pushing avant-garde or outsider voices into the mainstream, we simply try to get those voices in a situation where, if anybody is interested, they can understand and engage, but they don't have to.

By "they don't have to" I mean we keep our budgets low and our egos in check so we can make movies that only need to succeed modestly for us to be profitable enough so we can show up the next year. We have to run this like a business, but we don't ever have to ask people to change what they're doing to force it into the mainstream.

And with *Woodstock*, tell me a bit about how you decided to handle Tiber's homosexuality and the Stonewall aspect of his book?

I really felt like coming at Elliot's gay identity from two directions. One was the specific, that is, his own story, and releasing that to the audience. But in addition, during the course of that Woodstock weekend he was also coming out to himself. It's not that he didn't have a gay identity, but it was very much closeted. So we respected the closet, but then we opened it up as he did himself. We're getting it at the same time as he his.

On the meta-movie side, having done *Brokeback*, where the key problem of the movie is kind of "Oh, my God, I'm gay!" to *Milk*, where the key issue was, "Oh, my God, you're homophobic!" where being gay wasn't the problem anymore, homophobia was, to *Woodstock*, where our main character's gay and so what? It's part of what he has to deal with, but he's the hero. So, he's gay. It's not like when they advertise *Paul Blart: Mall Cop* they advertise it as "this summer's new straight comic hero." It's like, okay, he's gay.

A nonissue?

It's an issue in that it was an issue for Elliot and we wanted that to be part of the movie. I think it's important, but it's not an issue in the sense that we're not waving a flag and that's what the movie's all about. No, it's just a movie where the hero's gay, and that's cool.

Independent film has reached an unprecedented popularity. It's become a true brand today and every major media conglomerate has an imprint in the market. This is a great thing because we get a much richer selection of films but it's a dangerous thing because of the potential corruption of the voice of this type of film.

Here's the thing. The overriding thesis of the question is challengeable on multiple touch points. One is the genealogy of it; that is to say, have you ever met someone who describes themselves as a *dependent* producer? So already you have an issue with what is indie and what isn't and you get into that whole discussion.

If you really wanna bore everyone around you and never have sex again in your life, just go to a party and say, "What is indie film?" At that point you're going in circles. If it's not the financing, is it the spirit? Does it have stars in it? Is it this? Is it that?

I don't use the word independent film. I'm in the specialized film business. I run a company that's part of a studio. So-called independent film is different than the avant-garde . . . At the very birth of independent film— that is to say *narrative* feature-filmmaking that was outside the studio system and that was more auteur-driven than star-driven—[Schamus buzzes through an effortlessly fluent, professorial recitation of seminal keys from Jean-Luc Godard and Monogram Studios to Roger Corman and Sam Arkoff to *Shadows* by John Cassavetes].

If you like narrative, which is the game we're in—
especially talking to the Writers Guild—then it gets
very interesting trying to trace what you mean by independent cinema. As opposed to what? Then you get
yourself into trouble thinking that the success of independent film has resulted in an inevitable decline of its
inner integrity as an outside voice that was challenging
the mainstream.

To the extent to which independent film always took
narrative seriously, it just had a different way of treating
narrative formulae—different images, voices, and politics, and those things. But 99.999 percent of the genetic
code that makes a successful independent movie, I hate
to tell ya—is the same as what makes a successful studio movie: It's called narrative.

**Without daring to even attempt to define independent
film—assuming I have no interest in sorting through that
genealogy and going instead with the simple idea that, "I
don't know how to tell you what it is, but I know it when I
see it"—has its success created things where you see independent film aping itself, at least in its marketing and its
aesthetic? At what point does that insinuate itself into the
creative, artistic product itself?**

Clearly it has to in some way. You're in a context. You're
walking into a situation that has a kind of protocol, you
might say. But then again there's this assumption that
there's this spectrum where on one end there's absolute

freedom and the other absolute sell-out. The fact is, I don't believe—well, maybe there is absolute sell out, but I think people would be so stupid to think they even could absolutely sell out and be successful.

The whole point is that your movie has to be different, so even that doesn't work. The absolute freedom end seems to me basically a private language spoken without any capital investment; it's a fantasy that drives itself as a kind of vanishing point for a lot of ego to lay claim to a certain kind of freedom or integrity.

The minute you're printing a call sheet that has a crew listed on it and you're using money . . .

You inherently no longer have absolute freedom.

But you know what? Absolute freedom is not a value. The value is [asking] "How can I make something that allows a certain kind of articulation in the world that really is different and that really has something to say? I'm gonna need resources to do that, so I'm going to need to speak a language"—let's call it a narrative language—"that gets people's attention and emotional investment. I'm not afraid of [using] emotion as a tool in my tool kit, therefore I'm no longer in the world of right and wrong because I can't be right always if I'm appealing to people's emotions. Therefore I'm going to take the craft of what I'm doing—let's say as a writer—

seriously and as something of value even though it's suddenly evacuated of any of the political pretentions I had three seconds ago."

People talk to me all the time and say, "Wow, you guys must have a pretty profound political agenda [with films like] *Motorcycle Diaries* and *Brokeback Mountain* and *Taking Woodstock*." I always say, "Whether I have an agenda or not, the key thing is that the movie better be good because otherwise it doesn't matter what your politics are."

INTERVIEWER
Do you have an agenda?

JAMES SCHAMUS
My agenda is, again, going back
to sufficient and necessary, I certainly don't want the films we do at
Focus to add to the pile of cultural
crap out there in the world. I would
rather that every film we do have
some articulating voice driving it;
somebody has something to say,
even if they're working in a totally
mainstream genre, it's gotta be the
addition of a voice that wouldn't
have otherwise been heard.

That doesn't mean that we're snobs.
We've made some pretty readily
identifiable genre-ready movies.
That's part of my job too, part of
my work on myself, when someone
comes in with something that feels
more mainstream than what we do
usually, I have to step back to see
if hey, there's a reason for that or
there's something cool about that.

You don't want to just make films from a different per-spective for the sake of a different perspective.

Exactly. There are a lot of new perspectives, but some of them are probably boring.

You're an executive and screenwriter and an academic. You've kept your life and your body of work highly diver-sified with things that, in some cases, a lot of people would consider at odds.

What's really interesting about that is you look at film and people say, "Wow, executive *and* screenwriter? That's bizarre!" But when you look at television, the TV writer-showrunner-executive makes total sense. It doesn't make total sense in my pocket of the film world because I'm living in a world that prizes a kind of auteurist ethos that really comes down to the director. That makes it a little more interesting for me. I get to drive the train, but I'm really just the engineer. I'm just shoving the coal in there.

AARON
SORKIN

CAREER HIGHLIGHTS:
The Social Network; Moneyball; The West Wing; A Few Good Men

"I tend to write people who are smarter than I am, smoother than I am, [and], in most tangible ways, better than I am."

—AARON SORKIN

If you're watching a movie that's not from the '40s or '50s and characters are saying really clever things, really fast, there's an excellent chance Aaron Sorkin wrote it. In an era where dialogue has become virtual anathema in mainstream film, Sorkin has built a giant, Oscar-winning career by writing some of the smartest and quickest around.

It was actually not feeling smart at dinner table debates growing up that drove him to screenwriting. With writing, Sorkin could control, edit, and perfect his thoughts in a way that seemed spontaneous.

He debunks two commonly held screenwriting myths: the idea that dialogue is to be jettisoned at every turn and the clichéd notion that a true artist stays up until all hours writing. *Bad* dialogue is the only problem with dialogue, he says. Go to bed and get some sleep, you'll write better.

You're kind of a Luddite.

That's not inaccurate.

So what attracted you to *The Social Network* initially?

What attracted me to it had nothing to do with Facebook. The invention itself is as modern as it gets, but the
story is as old as storytelling; the themes of friendship,
loyalty, jealousy, class, and power. This is story that
Aeschylus would have written or Shakespeare or Paddy
Chayefsky. Luckily for me, none of those guys were
available, so I got to do it.

They didn't call in Aeschylus for a punch up?

They were gonna call in Aeschylus for a polish, but I
swore I could do it myself, so they called him off.

**You've said that story is harder for you, that what you love
is dialogue. To what extent did this whole Facebook thing
provide you with that skeletal structure on which to embel-
lish theme and work your magic with dialogue?**

You still have to find Waldo in there somewhere. Here's
how it started: I got a fourteen-page book proposal that
Ben Mezrich had written for his publisher for a book he
was going to call *The Accidental Billionaires*. The publisher was simultaneously shopping it around for a film
sale. That's how it wound up in my hands. I was reading

it and somewhere on page three I said, "Yes." It was the fastest I'd said yes to anything.

But Ben hadn't written the book yet, and I assumed that Sony was gonna want me to wait for Ben to write the book and that I would start a year from now. Instead, they wanted me to start right away. Ben and I were kind of doing our research at the same time, sort of along parallel lines.

Was he sending you pages as he went?

No. Two or three times we'd got together—I'd go to Boston or we'd meet in New York and kinda compare notes and share information, but I didn't see the book until he was done with it. By the time I saw the book I was probably 80 percent done with the screenplay.

So, there's a lot of available research and I also did a lot of first-person research with a number of the people that were involved in the story. I can't go too deeply into that because most of the people did it on the condition of anonymity. But what I found was that two lawsuits were brought against Facebook at the roughly same time, that the defendant, plaintiffs, witnesses all came into a deposition room and swore under oath, and three different versions of the story were told. Instead of choosing one and deciding that's the truest one or choosing one and deciding that's the juiciest one, I decided to dramatize the idea that there were three different versions of the story being told. That's how I came up with the structure of the deposition room [which Sorkin uses as a narrative frame from which to tell the story in chronological sequence].

A lot is being written about your unflattering portrayal of Mark Zuckerberg, including a huge piece in the _The New Yorker_. How would you characterize your depiction of him?

I would say for the first hour and fifty-five minutes of the movie, he is an anti-hero and for the final five minutes, he's a tragic hero. In order to be a tragic hero you have to have paid a price and you have to feel remorse. I would say both of those things are true at the end of the movie. I think that what we see is a very brilliant guy, a terribly complicated guy, but also a guy who is very angry because he kind of lives with his nose pressed up against the window of social life. As a result, he did something extraordinary—he reinvented social life so that he and other people could reinvent themselves.

This is a bit psychoanalytical, but I read that you felt somewhat inconsequential as a conversationalist at times, early on in life, and that writing gave you a voice that mattered. You and Zuckerberg could not be more different, but are there any correlations between you in terms of the way he reframed the situation to matter?

I think what you're referring to is that when I was growing up, I was surrounded with friends and family, by people that were smarter than I was. I'm not quite sure why they had me around. I think I was the mascot or something. I really loved the sound of smart argument.

In my house growing up, anyone that used one word when they could have used ten just wasn't trying.

I also was taken by my parents to see plays, and often I was too young to understand what was going on onstage, but I loved the sound of dialogue. It sounded like music to me, and I wanted to be able to imitate that. So as a writer now, I tend to write people who are smarter than I am, smoother than I am, and in most tangible ways, better than I am. There is a corollary with what goes on in social networking. When someone does a status update, posts something on someone's wall, they're not talking, they're not being conversational—they've done a rewrite and a polish and they're putting forward the version of themselves that they want you to see.

They're putting forward the shooting draft.

Exactly.

And there is that other aspect of Zuckerberg being not so socially confident . . .

Yeah, it was important to me in writing Mark that I locate the parts of myself that I felt were like him. I also, as with a lot of people, have felt and do feel socially awkward and nervous in a lot of situations, not smooth. But the difference is, and I want to be clear: I've never met or spoken to Mark Zuckerberg . . .

Right.

So I'm talking about the character of Mark Zuckerberg in the movie. These are things that made Mark deeply angry and those are things that never made me angry, they just gave me a way to write.

How much time did you spend on this script from stem to stern?

You know, this movie went so smoothly. From the day that I got that fourteen-page book proposal to the day I delivered the script to Sony was a year. It was May when I delivered it, the following October we were shooting it, and this October 1, it hits theaters.

And that initial draft, I've learned from the Internet, was 161 pages?

One hundred and sixty-two pages. So was the shooting script. No pages were cut. The first thing David Fincher did when he came to the studio was say, "This script isn't long." The first I worked with David, he came to my house with a stopwatch and he said, "I want you to read out loud every scene at the pace you heard it when you were writing it." And he would time each scene.

He'd say, "Okay, the first scene with Mark and Erica, five minutes, seven seconds." And when we got into rehearsal, when Jessie and Rooney [Mara, who plays the object of Zuckerberg's affections] were running through that scene, if it wasn't five-o-seven, if it was five forty-three, he'd say, "No, this scene plays at five-o-seven." That's how a 162-page screenplay is an hour-and-fifty-seven-minute movie.

You must have said, "Hallelujah!"

I did. There were any number of things David did to which I said "Hallelujah!"

Yes, but this is your famous Aaron Sorkinness finding a perfect home.

Yes, for better or for worse.

INTERVIEWER

You don't stay up late to write any
more, you write in the morning now.
Has that had any discernible effect
on your work?

AARON SORKIN

I don't think so. I was worried that
it was going to. There seems to be
something romantic and bohemian
and edgy about staying up all night
and writing and I was worried that
once I stopped doing that it would
homogenize my writing somehow. It
turned out the time of day had nothing to do with it.

So that's largely a fantasy of that image of the struggling artist, living in the wee hours?

Yeah.

So go to sleep and get up and write some good stuff?

Yeah. A writer will generally have a sweet spot when they have energy and the ideas are all in the right place. Listen, the thinking doesn't stop. When I go to bed at night, my mind is still racing. I'm thinking a lot about what it is I'm going to write tomorrow. If I don't know what I'm going to write tomorrow, I have a lot of anxiety about it. If I do know, I'm very excited about it. But it's when I get up in the morning that I have the most energy and that's usually when most of the writing gets done. It doesn't just happen in the morning. I write in the afternoon and the evening, I'm just not writing at 1:00 A.M. anymore.

Nearly every screenwriting teacher and how-to book warns against over writing dialogue, yet some of our most gifted screenwriters—Quentin Tarantino and Woody Allen among them—specialize and indulge in dialogue. Do you think that the rule should be, "Don't write dialogue unless you're really good at it"? Is there something false about that rule?

That rule is completely false. It's espoused by people who don't write dialogue very well. There are thousands of ways to tell a story. Some people do it more visually than others. I'm a guy that writes people talking in rooms. Some people, like Harold Pinter, are minimalist when it comes to dialogue but they write brilliant dialogue, just a different kind. This business of jettisoning dialogue—I feel like that's something a B-action star would say.

NICHOLAS
SPARKS

CAREER HIGHLIGHTS:
The Notebook (novel); *A Walk to Remember* (novel); *The Last Song* (novel and screenplay)

"Writing the screenplay is easier for me, quite frankly. It's not as long and once you understand the screenplay structure, it's simply writing."

—NICHOLAS SPARKS

If Nicholas Sparks were a character in one of his bestselling novels, he'd be the athletically handsome writer from hardscrabble beginnings who made millions spinning his woe over a lost love into tales that touched the hearts of women everywhere.

In reality only the athletically handsome, pauper-turned-millionaire, bestselling novelist bits are true . . . oh, and the part where he's touched the hearts of millions of women (and men) around the world.

But that's where the similarities end.

The author of *The Notebook* and *A Walk to Remember* is a happily married father of five, and a man of military precision, unabashed self-confidence, and massive drive. He's more over-achiever than lovesick romantic lead, really.

He rises at 5:30 A.M., works out several hours each day, coaches track, and has funded and built a Christian school in his community in North Carolina—all while producing no less than 2,000 words a day.

Had he not been catapulted to millionaire status by *The Note-book* in 1996 (he'd promised himself he'd be a millionaire before he was thirty and just made the cutoff by a few months), he says he would have been a hedge-fund manager. As a writer he's an autodi-dact; he studied business finance in college.

So, guys, if you think being a sensitive, artistic type means you're destined for a successful writing career, Sparks is evidence that a ton of hard work is also fairly crucial.

Here he chats about the film *The Last Song*—the first time he wrote a screenplay *before* he wrote the novel. He says every novel is a struggle. He actually doesn't outline his novels or screenplays, and he explains why, when he's writing a script, he starts every scene at the end.

Surely this must have been a different experience from a writing standpoint to write the novel after having written a screenplay?

Yes and no. I suppose my biggest disappointment was that after finishing the screenplay, which was about 105 pages or so, I thought writing the novel would be easier. It was not. It was as hard as every novel I've ever written.

Not harder or less hard?

Not harder or less hard. All novels I write are exceptionally challenging.

So it's usually a struggle?

It is very much a struggle.

INTERVIEWER
What is the hardest part for you?

NICHOLAS SPARKS
The hardest part for me goes hand
in hand with the genre in which I
work. In many genres you read these
stories because you know what to
expect in terms of voice and structure and pacing. Elements of the
story might be different, but the
structure and voice and pacing tends
to be the same. People read a lot of
different authors because they like
the way these elements are handled.

In my particular genre it's impera-
tive to vary the voice, the pacing,
and the structure as well as the
story because people read them to be
surprised. Every time I sit down to
write, it feels like I'm reinventing the
wheel all over again. So I've had novels I've written in first person, I've
combined first and third person, I've
written in third person, I've written
in limited third person omniscient.
I have written long novels, short

novels, and medium novels. I have
written novels with many characters
and novels with only a few characters. I have written novels from the
point of view of a woman, from a
man, from an eighty-year-old man,
from a twenty-nine-year-old divorced
female, to a soldier to, in this particular case, a seventeen-year-old girl.

But as unique as all those variations are, it's also always sort of the Nicholas Sparks love story that's anticipated.

Of course, there is always a love story element in there. It's always a story in which most of the emotions are covered. It is a story that's always set in North Carolina, always in a small town, so there are some things that are the same, but the main challenges with writing go down to things like character, voice, structure, pacing, and story. So I have to vary those every time I sit down to write.

Have you ever longed to get out of North Carolina or the love story frame?

Not necessarily, because I have to vary so much, I'm allowed to incorporate elements of other genres in my work. For instance, I can incorporate danger or mystery and that helps keep what I write different and unique.

Did the writing of this particular screenplay teach you anything about writing in general?

Writing the screenplay is easier for me, quite frankly. It's not as long, and once you understand the screenplay structure, it's simply writing. I attempt to do the same thing [as I do with novels]. I attempt to move the reader to green-light the movie.

How much are you a structured outliner with your novels?

I don't outline at all.

So in that sense, the screenplay, with its strict skeletal structure, is different, right?

It was. There's no question it was different—that there are different rules that come into play. Narrative in a screenplay, for instance, tends to be much easier because you're allowed to tell, you don't have to show because the actor is going to show the emotion. You can write, "She entered the house still angry from her argument with Will." I can write that in a screenplay, I can't write that in a novel. I have to write, "She came in the house and slammed the door and windows shook," or whatever. You have to show it.

At the same time, in novels it's an easier flow of dialogue because you can start at the beginning whereas with screenplays, you almost start every scene at the end.

You start every scene at the end of the scene?

Of course. In the sense of dialogue and action, because if you try to start them from the beginning of the scene as in a novel, it would take too long to get to the point of that scene. So assumptions are made in screenplays, whereas, in novels, generally you have to work the truth of the backstory into the novel itself.

With your novel writing you don't outline, you just have it in your head.

Correct.

With the screenplay did you take the same approach?

Yes.

When you were writing in relative obscurity, you were working in pharmaceutical sales?

Yes.

And you had completed several novels in your spare time. You had submitted *The Notebook* [to agents] but hadn't heard much back yet. What kind of attitude did you cultivate about the work when you hadn't had success? How much do you feel that had to do with your ultimate success? Does that make sense?

The question makes sense; however, you're a tiny bit misinformed, which is fine. Let me answer that by saying this—when I wrote *The Notebook*, I liked the story. I thought that if I did it well, it would be a story that moved people; it would be a story that people would remember for a very long time. I don't know if I'm any different than any other author who's working on their novel, but I was very confident that it was a good story.

And yet, I was fully aware that it's a very challenging environment. There are no guarantees in publishing. So I guess you could say that I was confident and that confidence was tinged with lots of hope and a part of me that said, "Well, maybe it's not going to work." How's that?

Great.

The first agent that read the manuscript took me on as a client. When I submitted it to publishers on Thursday, it had sold by Monday noon. So it wasn't necessarily a long and grueling process. But by the same time, even once it sold, there was no guarantee people were going to buy if from the stores. So you have an entire year in which you hope it's going to work, but you really can never expect it to work.

SYLVESTER STALLONE

CAREER HIGHLIGHTS:

Both the *Rocky* and *Rambo* franchises; *The Expendables;*
Paradise Alley

"I believe in writing the first draft very quickly, putting
it down for two weeks, going back to rework it, then
putting it down for three or four days and so on. That
way, you can't wait to get back to it, you're revitalized."
—SYLVESTER STALLONE

Sylvester Stallone isn't a lot of people. From his troubled youth as
an under-tended, mush-mouthed outsider (he suffered facial paraly-
sis at birth due to a forceps mishap), through lean, rejection-filled
early years in Hollywood, the sixty-year-old writer, director, and actor
is actually, with no irony, a kind of real-life Rocky. He is the unlikely
nobody who, in real life, won against long odds.

Flash to pre-*Rocky* days: Stallone was dangling over a very
real chasm of existential oblivion. He was penniless with a pregnant wife. Despite having acted in a few things and even written
1974's *The Lords of Flatbush*, his home was a tiny L.A. apartment
with no phone.

So, not being a lot of people, he painted his windows black and
wrote a boxing movie.

When he was eventually offered six figures for the resulting script,
he again did what no starving, desperate person would: He turned
them down until they agreed to let him star in the film as well.

What is rarely acknowledged about Stallone is what a good screenwriter he is. He not only won the best picture Oscar for *Rocky* in 1977 (beating out *Taxi Driver* and *Network*), but was nominated as an actor and screenwriter, putting him in a club whose only other members were Charlie Chaplin and Orson Welles.

He's the kind of writer that, no matter how you feel about his sixth Rocky film *Rocky Balboa*, when you see his aging fictional champ, you don't wonder why he's there, you wonder how he's been.

During a frank, in-depth conversation, Stallone talks about his film *Rocky Balboa*, getting older, and Rocky's surprising connection to Charlie Chaplin. He says that walking away from a screenplay for a few weeks is crucial to let fresh ideas percolate to improve it.

If you're having trouble focusing, do what he did to write *Rocky*: Turn off all the clocks and paint your windows black.

I've gotta start with the obvious question: What motivated you to revisit the Rocky story at this stage?

Two reasons: I wasn't satisfied with the ending of *Rocky V*. I felt it was unfulfilling to both me and the audience. It didn't really signify the last chapter in his life.

Time passed and people moved on to different things. My life went through a series of changes. I began to reflect on what it's like to be a certain age and what's up ahead and what's been behind, and I thought a lot of people must feel that, right? Their salad days are behind them but deep down inside they still feel that they're competitive, that they have another mountain to climb.

They've got something "left in the basement" [a line from *Rocky Balboa*]?

Exactly, something in the basement. And also, as you get older, you're confronted with loss in a way that you might not be in your twenties or thirties. Real loss: loss of friendship, loss of loved ones, loss of opportunity. That really does add into the equation of how one looks at his final chapters in life, you know?

Through the four other *Rocky* sequels and all the other action films you've done, including the *Rambo* franchise, I think filmgoers started thinking more about the formula.

Yeah, that does happen. I think enough time has passed that I forgot the formula by now [*laughs*].

But I have to say, *Rocky Balboa* is unlike middle sequels in the way it reminds you just how rich a character this is, that there is more story to be told with him.

I'm glad you like it 'cuz I was a little worried that perhaps the audience has changed. Well, here's the dilemma: The audience *has* changed, and the question is, are they patient for the written word like they were years ago? In the '70s there was a whole different taste for film. Then I thought, you know, "I can't think about that. Let me write for the people that enjoyed the first one. Let me write the age-appropriate *Rocky*. Let's not be glib or try to install situations or music or anything that tries to bring a new audience on." If they like the film—and I hope they do—they will for the same reasons they liked the first one.

Did you struggle with how to end this fight?

Oh, yeah, very much so. I shot it three ways . . . and I thought, you know, this is not about winning. Even if he wins, he's never going to fight again. This is about catharsis. He needed to purge himself physically. Like he says earlier in the movie, "I need to replace old pain with new pain." He's always going to feel pain. I believe that in life we live with conditions. That's never gonna go away. I mean, if your heart's been broken, it's always gonna be a little broken.

I've read that you like to write fast, so you write fast but you're a big rewriter?

Unbelievable. You have no idea.

Well give me an idea. How many drafts did you do with this film?

I would say like twenty. I love to rewrite, I really do. What happens is I'll start just working a scene and I'll touch up that dialogue and add a little situation here and then it grows.

I also ask myself, if there was no dialogue, what could I do to make this scene more interesting? An example is the scene where Rocky goes to the graveyard. How do I say he goes there a lot? I don't want him saying, "You know, I go to this graveyard every day." So I gave him a wooden folding chair that he puts back up in a tree when he leaves. That says that he lives in the graveyard.

You know this might sound kind of silly, but there is a Chaplinesque quality to the way you handle Rocky.

You just nailed it. Charlie Chaplin is what I've always equated this character to. He's a pugilistic Charlie Chaplin—the Little Tramp.

When I was putting this movie together, I didn't want Rocky to look the same, so I didn't want him to wear the hat [he wore in the original movie]. We went through different hats, wool hats, baseball hats, and the character just wasn't coming alive. Then I thought of Charlie Chaplin. Would he have ever changed his hat from a derby to say a straw hat? It would have killed the character. So as much as I didn't want to do it, I wore the hat. It's just all part of the character.

Rocky's hat is like a fedora, right?

They call it a "stingy brim."

Why do they call it a "stingy brim"?

Because there's not much of a brim.

Right.

There's a small little two-inch brim. Rocky would call it a "stingy brim lid."

INTERVIEWER

Let's go back in time to before you wrote *Rocky*, when you were struggling in the mid-'70s in L.A. What kind of screenwriting training did you take?

SYLVESTER STALLONE

Very little. I would go to the films a lot and I would go home and try to do a parody of that film. If it was a western, I'd try to write a couple scenes of a western with my own dialogue, which was usually not very good. But that's how I did it initially, with a sort of mimicry. I never had any training in the professional way. But after a while you start to learn.

The most important rule that I've learned as a screenwriter is that you've gotta put [a script] down for two weeks. Just let it get cold and then revisit it. Something percolates in the subconscious and you come back with so many more ideas.

If I were to just sit there and rework
a scene over and over I don't get
time for new ideas to incubate. I
believe in writing the first draft
very quickly, putting it down for
two weeks, going back to rework it,
then putting it down for three or
four days and so on. That way, you
can't wait to get back to it, you're
revitalized.

Back in the '70s, before you wrote *Rocky*, what kind of shape were you in financially?

I literally had to sell my dog to a fella who owned a gym for like $30. That was Butkus.

As in Dick Butkus [the dog that later appeared in *Rocky* as the fighter's film dog]?

Yeah, the dog was named after Dick Butkus . . . I remember it very, very well.

And your wife was pregnant?

Yeah, just pregnant.

I've heard these stories of you painting the windows in your apartment black?

That was for concentration. Sometimes you look outside, it's a beautiful day and you say, "I'd like to maybe go out for a walk." I thought, "Let me just not even know what time it is." So I didn't even have a phone. I'd just write. Sometimes it would be 3:00 in the morning, sometimes 7:00—I never knew. I guess it was sorta like being in a Vegas casino gambling.

Except they weren't pumping oxygen in.

No, they certainly weren't.

Your actual real-life story is a rich one. You had a rough childhood, you weren't always healthy, you didn't get a lot of attention from your parents at times, and had trouble with other kids. Do you buy into this notion that this type of rough life experience lends a person the sensitivity and observational skill to write?

Absolutely. I believe it to a point. I don't believe you have to be maligned or thrown in a closet or completely deprived of all love, but I do believe that if everything is accomplished for you, you don't develop a point of view or hunger or even an insecurity that requires you to do something like writing.

I think most writers and painters are never satisfied with their work. And you say, "What is it? There's still stuff in the basement. What is it?"

And it's insecurity?

That's what I think it is. Imagine if you came from a home where there was nothing but love, everything was taken care of, and you were told you're the greatest. I don't know. What would motivate you to do anything?

MIKE
SWEENEY

CAREER HIGHLIGHTS:

Conan; *Late Night with Conan O'Brien*; *The Tonight Show with Conan O'Brien*

"We just go by the old rule of, if we're laughing, it's funny. Although sometimes we will rehearse stuff I know is going to get cut. But we do it for ourselves . . . And sometimes it gets on, which is a grave mistake."

—MIKE SWEENEY

Planning is not a tool in Mike Sweeney's kit. Despite working in the blood-drenched trenches of the late night–talk show ratings wars, the senior *Conan* writer has never really thought much of worrying, either.

Through O'Brien's thrilling move to the big time as host of *The Tonight Show with Conan O'Brien*, to the brutal, humbling fiasco that ensued, Sweeney remained unfazed by what became perhaps the goriest of all the late night–chat brawls.

In a conversation amid the *Tonight Show* mayhem that ultimately saw O'Brien fired from the iconic show he'd always dreamed of hosting, Sweeney is downright laid-back. He has the calm of a man who has already jumped into the abyss.

Indeed, Sweeney started his career in comedy with such a leap, when, without a dime of savings, he abandoned a Rutgers law degree and a career as a young Manhattan trial attorney to become a stand-up comic making fifty bucks a week.

After a stint as the warm-up comedian on *The Maury Povich Show*, he applied unsuccessfully to be a writer on the fledgling *Late Night with Conan O'Brien* in the early '90s. He didn't get the gig but was offered a slot as the show's warm-up comedian, which eventually led, in 1995, to a full-time writing post.

It was no kind of plan; he just kept being funny.

"I don't know what I'm doing after this phone call," Sweeney quips dryly and a little too convincingly. Here he speaks about the power of not planning, not writing jokes that are too local, and how writers on a show like *Conan* do it all.

And when the bullshit around you gets crazy, just ignore it and be funny.

You have been through a number of unexpected changes in your career. From a writing perspective, how have you found this experience of changing coasts and time slots with Conan?

It hasn't been that different, actually. It's been the same . . . *kind of.* We're doing five shows a week and NBC has always trusted Conan, so there's never been network interference, even now.

Even amid all the scrutiny of the new time slot and all the press?

Yeah, I dunno. I don't even feel the scrutiny I think because I just kind of walk into the building every morning and then leave at night. Plus I'm not very bright, so I'm not able to perceive when there's danger afoot.

There could be people screaming fire and pointing at you.

Exactly. The idea of higher scrutiny seems abstract to me in a way.

In the simplest terms, what was the game plan? I know you're not a game-plan guy.

My god, you've already got me nailed!

But was the game plan in the writers' room fundamentally the same, like, "Let's not revamp everything. Let's do what got us here"?

> We've definitely worked on coming up with new pieces for the *Tonight Show*. It was a good opportunity to do different things just for change's sake. All the writers who moved from New York, you know, have been there a while, so it's a good team and it just seemed like the natural thing to do.

So that writing unit remains the same but with the new opportunities presented by the new locale?

> Right. I think we looked at moving out here the same way we have when we've traveled the show. We'd go to Chicago, San Francisco, or Toronto in February and we'd always get very excited. It's very stimulating to do something different. I think it really energized all the writers. We looked at moving to L.A. in the same way. It's just a new location and all the things that come with that. It provides a lot of new opportunities for new ideas, so it's been fun.

Because so many of the writers are from New York, has it been difficult to grapple with the tone of jokes now that you're in L.A.? Even though it's a national show, have you had to check yourselves at all?

> The only thing we do, which we did on the old show, is not to have the L.A. jokes be too local. We try to avoid jokes about reservoir bonds in L.A. County, for example. We tried to be the same way in New York.

Are there new parameters as far as the tone of the mono-logue jokes or the bits, which have always been, how shall I say, outside the box? I mean, Michael McDonald Summer Camp and Masturbating Bear. Need I say more?

> Michael McDonald Summer Camp? Wow! Excellent.

This is a personal favorite with my crew.

> That's an example of how a lot of the sketch stuff is written and produced by an individual, or teams of writers. A lot of the writers perform on the show as well, and that's always been the case.

> If you write something, you don't hand it off to a production team. I mean, as far as producing it, writing it, and editing it, the writer does all of that. They get all the glory if it's great, and if it's not, you can still blame someone else.

INTERVIEWER

Has there been any need to make
things less weird for the earlier time
slot?

MIKE SWEENEY

I think we just try to stick to stuff
that makes us laugh because otherwise you lose your bearings if you're
trying to second guess whether something is appropriate for a certain time
of day. I don't even know how you figure something like that out.

We just go by the old rule of, if we're
laughing, it's funny. Although sometimes we will rehearse stuff I know
is going to get cut. But we do it for
ourselves.

For your souls.

> For our souls. And sometimes it gets on, which is a
> grave mistake.

**But none of this pressure in the press about Leno and you
and David Letterman and you, and the ratings and all that
stuff—none of that insinuates itself into the writers' room
and makes people get uptight? Does it get in there at all?**

> I try not to let it. I don't watch other shows, because I
> don't think that's a healthy thing to do. You don't want
> to be influenced by what somebody else is doing and
> also, I don't have any time. I don't have the time to
> watch any TV.
>
> So I just kind of block that stuff out because it's nothing
> I have any control over. Getting into that external stuff
> that's going on is kind of like empty calories in a way,
> so I don't get into it. Just putting the show on is so time
> consuming, I don't really have time to get into all this
> exterior stuff. It's kind of simple.

EMMA
THOMPSON

CAREER HIGHLIGHTS:
Sense and Sensibility; *Wit*; *Nanny McPhee*

"The first rule is: there is no inspiration. The only inspiration there is, is pulling up your chair, putting out a piece of paper, and starting to write. That's all there is."

—EMMA THOMPSON

The elegant British tones of Emma Thompson's speech make her comparison of comedy to sex seem altogether proper.

"One way of describing comedy has to do with the sexual act," she begins. "With men, jokes are to do with a building up to a climax and then the joke's over. Whereas female comedy tends to be much more circular, with no end and no beginning, and all sorts of little climaxes of laughter in the middle."

As her words float in the air she adds, "It's like the female orgasm."

This is the preamble to a fairly wonkish discussion of the screenwriting craft, upon the release of her film *Nanny McPhee*, which she wrote and starred in. Though she's far more famous as an actress than as a writer, she quickly reveals herself to be a seriously wise scripter. Her maiden screenplay was no modest affair: 1995's hugely successful adaptation of Jane Austen's classic *Sense and Sensibility*.

Pearls of wisdom include the idea that screenwriting is a little like painting in the sense that good work needs to be layered. She also insists that a properly written script needs to be fundamentally well constructed so it can take the necessary machinations involved in shooting it.

But above all, she says she has no easy rules: the only way to learn how you best write screenplays is to get to it!

The first screenplay you ever wrote was the adaptation of Jane Austen's *Sense and Sensibility*. I don't know how many people are aware of you as a writer; tell me how that job came to you?

> It was because Lindsay Doran, the producer, had seen my early BBC show [in 1988 Thompson wrote a six-episode comedy series for the BBC]. We also were working together at the time on *Dead Again*, and she just said, "Ha, would you be interested in adapting Jane Austen?" and I said, "Yeah, I'll give it go."

> I remember I started writing in the summer and it was a lovely summer so the first draft was written in a garden and it was about 700 pages long. I'd rung up a writer friend and asked, "How do you adapt?" and she'd said, "Well, just dramatize the whole book, see what works, and pare down and distill from there." Very good advice, actually. Four years later it was ready. Seventeen drafts.

Seventeen drafts?

> Oh, so many, yeah.

Was there any terror in the fact that this is Jane Austen and you're British?

> Yeah, completely. It was a little bit like when I stopped doing sketch acting and moved into "acting acting."

The first time I did it, I realized it's the same thing only longer.

Were there any resonating lessons about the screenwriting process that you took from that maiden voyage?

Yes, definitely. There are things I've applied later and always apply for *me*. Not general lessons, because you can't give anyone lessons. I think you have to not know what the hell you're doing and get on with it and see how you do it. Do you know what I mean?

You've got to find your own individual road?

Totally. And the first rule is: there is no inspiration. The only inspiration is pulling up your chair, putting out a piece of paper, and starting to write. That's all there is.

The next thing with screenplays is that it's a layering process. I do really think that's true; I think that screenplays are a very peculiar form and they take a long time to develop because it's not just about words as much because there are very few.

It's spare.

It's very spare.

So you mean the layering of structure, character . . .

Structure, character, *tone* being one of the most important and difficult things. You will find that each version
you write will have a particular tone. You need to do
many, many rewrites because then the tone starts to
become layered.

In literal terms, you'll keep some things from the first
draft all the way through and in the end you might find
that you've only kept one speech because that one speech
has always been right. It's such a fascinating process.

Like painting?

Yeah, it is a little bit like that because once you hand it
over, it's got to be able to hold water. That's what I mean
by structure; it's got to be put together so well that you
can put it into all sorts of positions in terms of where
you set it, where's the lighting, who are the actors—
there're so many things. [And] so many screenplays are
not well enough constructed and they just fall apart in
your hands as soon as you start moving them around.

INTERVIEWER

What do you find to be the most difficult part of the writing process?

EMMA THOMPSON

It's knowing when to end scenes,
I think. And the other really vital
thing is knowing that every character has to have a different voice. One
of the biggest problems with screenplays is that people don't bother to
differentiate between the different
ways each character speaks.

All the characters sound like the screenwriter?

Exactly.

When had you first become exposed to the source material for *Nanny McPhee*?

When I was about six or seven?

And apparently it stuck with you.

It definitely stuck with me.

Had you always planned on revisiting *Nanny McPhee* as an adult or did it just sort of pop up again accidentally?

I just picked it up one day when I was cleaning up at home and I read it and rang Lindsay and said, "There's this strange book I found," and I described the premise and she asked me to send it to her. She wound up saying "Let's do it!" And that's where our problems started [*laughs*].

What in this story appealed to you?

I think it was the character of Nanny McPhee; it was this very, very ugly character who changes in relation to other peoples' behavior, the alchemical nature of her methods. I love transformations.

So the transformation and the debunking of superficial beauty?

> Yeah, exactly. She's absolutely beautiful and kind always, but how she's perceived is the clue. You don't know whether it's a trick of the light, or of perception, or whether she's actually changing or even there at all, actually.

Because the source material for this is so limited, I assume one of your biggest challenges with the screenplay was . . .

> Yeah, writing the story. That was the challenge. There's no structure, or narrative, there's just a series of vignettes.

So a lot different from the work you did when you started out on *Pride and Prejudice*?

> Yes, exactly so. Most of this is original. I mean the story is me.

GUS
VAN SANT

CAREER HIGHLIGHTS:

Drugstore Cowboy; *My Own Private Idaho*; *Elephant*

"By the time I was writing *Drugstore Cowboy*, the writing was the most enjoyable part because you could do whatever you wanted—you weren't filming . . . You can invent huge, difficult-to-execute things. You have a lot of time to think about it and relax and let other people read it. It's sort of the most comfortable period."

—GUS VAN SANT

Much like his films, Gus Van Sant is soft-spoken, poetic, and almost purposefully enigmatic. Though he has helmed several mainstream projects like *Good Will Hunting* and *Drugstore Cowboy*, he's most acclaimed by critics and fans alike for his signature, structure-defying work outside the norm. Films like *My Own Private Idaho*, *Elephant,* and the much-loved, much-hated *Gerry* represent the film-maker as a writer, director, and reimaginer of the film form.

In a wide-ranging discussion centered on his film *Last Days*, based on the days leading up to the shotgun suicide of grunge-godhead Kurt Cobain, Van Sant talks about not considering himself a writer, but how the craft has come to be one of his favorite aspects of filmmaking.

He also discusses ad-libbed dialogue versus written dialogue and his love for toying with the very foundations of narrative structure like dialogue and conflict.

Increasingly your films like *Elephant, Gerry*, and *Last Days* have relied on cinema vérité style of ad-lib dialogue . . .

That's a really good thing to talk about for a Writers Guild piece.

Well, right, but I'm curious about it because you've done both [scripted dialogue and ad-libbed].

I'd seen other movies where people do that, like [Andy] Warhol movies, where everybody's basically just saying whatever they wanted. There were some great things that came out of that. I think I was very familiar with that style of pop-artsy films . . . [John] Cassavetes did stuff that, whether he wrote it down or not, the way they rehearsed it, it seemed like it was all being made up.

I guess I had done things with other movies where characters did make stuff up. In *Drugstore Cowboy* and *My Own Private Idaho* we always had scenes where people made stuff up, but meanwhile there was a script that we were shooting.

What's the appeal of this style for you artistically?

I think the overriding interest is to make something that resembles the way we live or think. There used to be all these rules of how to do things that slowly get eaten away by innovations that usually make the experience "life-like." It's all part of trying to get something that's more representative of our lives. That's usually what guides me and probably a lot of people.

There are conventions that we stick with almost stubbornly because we also want it to be like a movie. We don't want it to be too real.

Real to a point.

Yeah, real to a point. So if you get rid of conflict, for example, you're getting rid of that first rule you learned about writing a story and you're hesitant about that because, all of the sudden you're not allowing the audience to be drawn into your story. They have to be drawn to the story by other means. But there's not necessarily conflict in our daily lives. I think in these three films, I do have large conflict, so I haven't really ditched conflict, but I'm always trying to play with it.

And in terms of the ad-libbed dialogue?

Yeah. If one author is writing it, you're sort of playing with a Shakespearean model; you're having this one author issue the voices for all the characters. Meanwhile, the actors are just meant to say the lines, they're not meant to change anything. With this approach, the actors themselves are the characters.

I'm not casting actors, I'm casting real people. So people can't do anything wrong. The things they say and do are right because they're separate from any senior voice that's issuing lines from on high. They're collaborating on it.

Did you have any kind of script with *Last Days*?

We had one that was very similar to the one we used on *Elephant*, which was a twenty-page piece that described each scene but didn't have dialogue unless there were things I just couldn't describe without it. So sometimes it did have dialogue, but there was never really the type of dialogue we're used to, which is back-and-forth dialogue, which is another sort of convention.

Is this a way you want to continue working?

I don't know if I can, you know? I think it depends on the project and what the guidelines are. I think I'll do different things, but I'm pretty fascinated with trying to cast real characters playing those parts, so, if you have a used car salesman, you cast a used car salesman, you don't cast Brad Pitt playing a used car salesman.

This seems like a part of an obvious cultural trend.

Really?

Well, it seems like increasingly, whether it's with realistic, less-scripted comedy stuff on cable, or mockumentary-style films or, of course, reality TV, that reality in general has a pretty obvious pop cultural appeal nowadays.

Yeah, that's true.

That's not to liken what you're doing to reality TV, but there is sort of this . . .

Yeah, there's a similarity.

. . . weird connection. Do *you* think it's part of a larger cultural trend?

I think the stuff that I'm doing is different in the sense that it's not meant to entertain you in the same way. I think reality TV came out of *The Real World* . . . Reality TV is essentially like a documentary. For some reason documentaries have taken this huge backseat to fictional films and all of the sudden it's like the American consumers' version of accepting documentaries into their world.

The person that was only ever watching sit-coms is suddenly fascinated by real stuff. I think a lot of documentary filmmakers just cannot watch fictional films, and they've always felt it's like jazz, you know? "Someday the consumers will turn to us," [they say], and in a certain way, that's sort of happening with these reality TV shows. Except it's sort of obnoxious because they're not making [these shows] with grace . . . they have to cut every five seconds and, I don't know . . .

And it's still sort of a fake reality.

Yeah. And they have the people talking in front of a backdrop about like, "I didn't know Shannon was going to pull this on me," [*laughs*] and then you show the scene. You always have this altered reality of them commenting on what happens later, which is a documentary technique, but it's used in a certain way in those programs that no documentaries would use.

What is *Last Days*? I know it's a fictional account in the shadow of the Kurt Cobain story, but what do you describe this film as?

Well, it's a fictional piece that is sort of taking off from a period of someone's life that is missing. There were these three days that are sort of missing in Kurt's life. He left rehab and then was found several days later. I don't remember the exact number of days, but I think three of the days are kind of a mystery [and] two of the days apparently he was just lying there already dead.

There was this sort of black hole of wondering where was he. It's looking at an area where there is no story and putting a story in. It's me imagining it, like a kind of anti-bio pic, where it's about something that was unknown as opposed to known.

INTERVIEWER
Because you're so visual, do you find scripting a chore?

GUS VAN SANT
As a filmmaker, when I was just starting out in my early twenties, I was a painter. I had written some things but I didn't really consider myself a writer and still don't really. But that's what I would do is write screenplays and study screenplays. I would go to AFI [American Film Institute] and read all the screenplays and write stories and there were a couple complete screenplays that I wrote that I never got going.

I was making short films, but they didn't occupy all my time, so otherwise I would spend time mapping out things that I wanted to do. I actually really enjoyed writing and learned to enjoy writing. By the time I was writing *Drugstore Cowboy*, the writing was the most enjoyable part because you could do whatever you wanted—you weren't filming. Filming was

always really difficult because you're
trying to control five or six things
at one time. You can invent huge,
difficult-to-execute things. You have a
lot of time to think about it and relax
and let other people read it. It's sort
of the most comfortable period.

You've said you like the Japanese philosophy that the first thought is the best thought. Do you apply this to scripting?

I do that, but I don't know if because I believe in it, it's just what I end up doing. I can apply a Zen principle to it, but it's not because it's Zen, it's because it's what ends up happening to me. Like the location that we got for *Last Days* is the first house we saw.

Is there a follow-up to your novel *Pink* in the works?

I've written on a couple different stories for a long time and I kind of hold back because they're not really ready. They're around, they just haven't been published.

You're rewriting them?

Yeah, going through and . . . I just never think they're ready.

That doesn't sound like you.

I know, I know. I'm not really a novelist, so I think part of it is that I'm learning to write. I'm still learning, so I do go over and over things. When I'm learning things, I do [that]. It's just when I feel like I've learned them that I can be a little more free and positive about what I'm doing, where I'm not afraid of the end result. In the case of this novel, I don't feel like it's finished . . . I haven't spent lots and lots and lots of time.

I think Ken Kesey described it as "hours and hours of meticulous carving," referring to one learning how to write and finding their voice and a position they're writing from. Once you have found that, it's amazing. That's what we usually read when we read great novels—artists that have found that.

ROB ZOMBIE

CAREER HIGHLIGHTS:

House of 1000 Corpses; *The Devil's Rejects*; *Halloween*

"Sure, I read a few of those books on how to write a screenplay, but most of those books are written by someone who's never written a good script. You look at the writer's credits and they've written one episode of *The Golden Girls* or something. People who write good scripts, write scripts. They don't write books about writing scripts."

—ROB ZOMBIE

There are zombies and then there are *Rob* Zombies. The latter is a type-A, multiplatinum hard rocker, movie producer, film composer, visual artist, and, yes, writer.

He is the original Renaissance Zombie.

He even briefly attended design school, but true to his hard-rock image, he hated it because the teachers were "talentless hacks." Still, behind the undead image, he's a smart, creative dude and a one-stop shop for film. He's written, directed, and done music for half a dozen films, including *House of 1000 Corpses* and *The Devil's Rejects*.

If you want to learn to write scripts, he says, jettison the bullshit how-to books by people who've never written anything good. Read some scripts you actually like, and get up super early.

How important is writing for someone as visual and musical as you are?

These days writing seems to be the only thing I ever do. It's what I spend most of my time on, it seems.

Is that a good thing? Do you enjoy it?

I love it. What I like about it is—you know I like to paint and draw too, and it's the same sometimes with music in the studio—it's that you can do it 100 percent by yourself. Writing can be done just as a total solo effort.

Do you find it hard?

Sometimes. It's like anything. You have good days and bad days.

But I mean, compared to music and the visual arts, which you seem to have a natural affinity for, was writing tougher to learn?

It definitely took more time to get a grasp on it. But it's also not as if it was entirely new to me . . . even though lyrics aren't anything like writing scripts, it's writing of a sort, [so] I'd been working with words in a fashion for a long time.

INTERVIEWER
How have you trained yourself to write?

ROB ZOMBIE
By studying other people's scripts and watching movies that appeal to me and asking, "Why do I like this? Why do I like that? Why does this work?"

Sure, I read a few of those books on how to write a screenplay, but, just like I told you with the school thing, once again, most of those books are written by someone who's never written a good script. You look at the writer's credits and they've written one episode of *The Golden Girls* or something. People who write good scripts, write scripts. They don't write books about writing scripts.

Looking at the scripts or the movies you like is really the only way you can do things. Everything begins because you're a fan of something.

Did you develop as a screenwriter between writing *House of 1000 Corpses* and *The Devil's Rejects*?

You really do develop a lot once you put [a script] into effect. You can write and write and write, but when you actually get to make a movie—and for me, especially being able to direct my own scripts—you can learn so much about what works and what doesn't. I think it's incredibly helpful. What could be better than working with the actor who's about to read the lines that you wrote? You can really see the script in action, how dialogue sounds.

The worst thing you can do with a script is make it sound written. What's great about *The Devil's Rejects* is that a lot of people think it's all ad-libs. That's flattering to me because I've always thought those are always the best scripts. To me, amateurish scripts sound like they've been written by somebody. It's not supposed to sound like that.

What's your actual process when it comes to writing time?

I do it on a computer. I've written on a notepad from time to time. I get up really early in the morning and just write until I feel like I'm done. I set the alarm for about 5:00 A.M.

Really? Rob Zombie wakes up at 5:00 in the morning?

Yeah, I love it. It's totally quiet and easy to focus. It's even before the sun's up, and the day hasn't started so there are no distractions.

So if you're getting up before dawn, what time are you going to sleep?

About 12:00 or 1:00. I don't need much sleep.